CHOOSING FULFILLMENT IS SCARY AF

GET UNSTUCK AND CHANGE THE LIFE YOU HAVE INTO THE LIFE YOU WANT

SARA STEPA

Editing: Yna Davis (www.publishwithpleasure.com)

Cover Design: Kasia Piatek (www.kasiapiatek.pl)

For my mama, who never stopped believing in me.

"Don't ask yourself what the world needs. Ask yourself what makes you come alive, and go do that, because what the world needs is people who have come alive."

— HOWARD THURMAN

CONTENTS

My Gift to You

Download your FREE Choosing Fulfillment Guide at www.theattitudeisgratitude.ca/yourguide.

This guide includes all of the practices and helpful tools I used to process my feelings about letting go of the life I knew to build a life I truly wanted.

In this guide, you are going to find practices and exercises to help you better understand what's holding you back from choosing the life you truly desire. You will find journal prompts, awareness techniques and specially curated Spotify playlists that vibe with each step of the process. Not to mention it's one of the most beautiful guides you've ever seen—but you gotta download it to believe it!

Once you have the guide in your hands, you can be more intentional about sitting down and doing the work when you want to.

Keep it on hand while you're reading or hunker down with some beats in the background. Either way is perfect if it feels good to you. When you use it doesn't matter, but using it is going to be *super helpful* in getting you the results you want. You can't get results without doing the work.

Introduction

Y ou're pumped. Life is great. You're at ease and in flow. Life is a freaking gift!

Or maybe it's not, and that's why you're here. I'm curious—when was the last time you felt that way, when you genuinely thought, *I love my life*? And no, sipping margaritas on a white-sand-beach vacation doesn't count. That's fleeting, but it can give you an idea of the feeling I'm talking about.

I'm guessing that if you're reading this, it's been a while since you've had those feelings, and it's probably been a minute since you felt excited about getting up in the morning. I've been there too, and I didn't even realize how out of sync I was or how long I had been there. It's *sooooo* easy to get caught up in the day-to-day, trying to stay on top of everything. We put so much pressure on ourselves to show up and perform that we forget to ask why we're doing it all in the first place. We forget that our lives are meant to be lived—aren't they?

If you're not feeling those pumped-up feels about

life, it's likely because you've forgotten that life is meant to be fulfilling. You might be overwhelmed with your workload or exhausted from trying to manage everyone's hockey, dance, tutoring, and work schedules. The drain from constantly bickering with your significant other is real, or maybe you're just tired of cleaning all the damn time. How many dishes can one person seriously make? (I ask myself this question at least once a week—and I live alone.) You're probably used to prioritizing all the things that you feel like you *should* be doing, and you've lost focus on the things you *want* to be doing. Been there!

There was a period in my life where I was doing pretty good. I was excelling in my career, to societal standards anyway, but I forgot to check in with myself about what I wanted and what made me feel good. I realized I wasn't feeling pumped about my so-called success. Instead, I felt drained. I was working so hard for the vision everyone else had for me, instead of the vision *I* wanted for me. What was the vision I had for me? I didn't even know.

Sound familiar?

Life is supposed to feel good. I mean, what's the point otherwise? What are you working so hard for if not to have a smile on your face at the end of the day? We make so many daily choices and life decisions from a place of necessity or for financial gain or to please other people, but we forget what's really important. We forget that life is meant to be lived and that we *can* choose a life that puts a smile on our face. You have the power to choose what you want. So I ask, why not choose fulfillment?

Okay, but what does that word actually mean? *"Fulfillment."* Is it about achievement? Happiness? What about success? E-commerce delivery, perhaps? (Not kidding with that last one. It legit pops up on Google!) Well, it could be all of the above, or none. It really depends because fulfillment is completely unique to you and can be felt in big or small ways. Again, *it is unique to you*.

Choosing fulfillment can look like a tonne of different things, but you have to ask yourself what it looks like in your life. What is it that you want but have been too afraid to ask for? What are you too scared to go after? What change is needed in your life to make you feel more like you? When stepping into a life you want, it's almost a guarantee that you will need to let go of part of the life you know, a part that is holding you back. What do you need to let go of? Choosing fulfillment might mean ending that unhappy marriage you've been holding on to for all the wrong reasons. Or it could mean going back to work—or *not* going back—after having kids. Perhaps you need to dump that lowlife of a partner you've been living with for four years—I mean, you can do better. Asking for that promotion, writing that book, taking a chance on that business, running that race, kicking that habit! It might even mean quitting your job. (Spoiler alert, that's what I did!) Choosing fulfillment could be anything, as long as it's right for you. What is it that you want but are too afraid to choose? If you've picked up this book, I'm willing to bet that you've been wrestling with your own big choice.

Fulfillment is something you will find when you're able to make a deeper and more meaningful connection to your life, where you are in tune with who you really are and what you truly desire. Fulfillment is not necessarily about happiness or joy, either, which can be a common misconception. I mean, no one ever said, "OMG, this cup of coffee is so fulfilling!" Right? It goes deeper. Fulfillment is felt when you are connected to who you really are and what you desire. It can bring feelings of peace, contentment, ease, alignment, and flow.

Fulfillment is a state of being. It's not just one single moment or something you pick up and put down when you want. Fulfillment is something you must actively choose, and choose over and over again. *Arrrgh*, I can hear your groans: "But that sounds like a lot of work!" Stay with me! You make choices every single day though, don't you? What you're going to wear, whether you drink coffee or tea, the office you walk into, the food you eat, the media you consume. These are *all* your own personal choices (and for the record, not making a choice is still a choice). Those were day-to-day examples, but we also make and commit to broader life choices every day as well, such as where we live, whether we have kids, what our relationship status is, or what job we have. We make choices all day every day. What makes the difference in getting and staying in that fulfilled state is making decisions that feel good to you, decisions that bring you closer to what *you* want. Notice how you make your decisions. How often are you making them out of habit, for other people, or out of expectation? When do you make choices for *you*? I'll say this with absolute authority: not enough! You do not choose yourself enough.

So before you take a big leap, start practicing! You can start right now. Practice choosing yourself with those day-to-day choices I mentioned above. The small things add up, and they're a good place to start to get used to choosing you. Keep practicing—you're worth it!

Deeper fulfillment, on the other hand, isn't about those general choices. Deeper fulfillment is going to require some transformational changes. If you're feeling out of sync and out of alignment, finding fulfillment will require you to shake up your life and to consciously choose something different. Something that might not "make sense" but will feel right for you. In order to reach that deeper feeling of fulfillment, you will need to step away from part of the life you know and step onto your own stage. It will require you to let go of the old and grab on to the new. The pages that follow will prepare you for that transformational choice, the area where you're ready to go all-in, the choice that is scary AF. This book isn't about choices in general; I'm not Brendon Burchard teaching you how to be a high-performer. I'm Sara Stepa, and my words are here to guide you toward that one big, super important, life-changing choice. I've got you. I walked through the scary things required for that kind of choice and I made it to the other side with no regrets—in fact, I wrote this book because of it.

If you are tired of living on autopilot and hear a whisper in your heart that is calling you for more, perk up those ears and listen! Let's prepare you to make a change and choose something different. Get your mind and soul ready to feel fulfilled and live a life you really want.

Trusting the Whisper

One day I was listening to a podcast about—you guessed it—fulfillment. As I listened to the episode, I found myself getting fired up, almost annoyed at the message coming across. Normally I'm pretty open to perspectives, and I can see where others are coming from. Not this time. I wholeheartedly disagreed with what I was hearing. The message coming through on this podcast was that people had to hit rock bottom before they would make changes in their lives. Something drastic had to happen to wake them up before they would take control. No! I don't believe that to be true at all. Why should we have to wait to fall apart to start again? I refused to believe that anyone has to hit rock bottom to make a change in their life.

Some experience those transformational life moments of hardship, loss, or addiction before they wake up, but that doesn't have to be you. No one should have to wait for their life to be in shambles before choosing something better. Despite experiencing a very emotional and low period that pushed me to make a change, I would not describe my low as being even close to rock bottom.

I was frustrated by the podcast's notion that those who had achieved success had either done so by "defying the odds" or because they hit a point so low that they had no other choice but to change. This is a common belief that is passed around the personal development and business realms. But what about you? What about the people who want to change but just don't know where to start? What about the people who just feel stuck? Can we not choose something different and change our lives without needing them to fall apart first? Of course we can. I know because I did it myself. I hit a tough spot before I found the strength and courage to step into my dreams. But I believe that anyone who has a dream on their heart or a whisper in their ear needs to listen and start leaning into the life they want. I don't want rock bottom to be the reason you finally decide to change your life, and I don't want you to wait for your life to become intolerable before you start making changes. A life of fulfillment is worth choosing, and it can be yours. The following pages don't tell you how great it feels to be fulfilled; they prepare you for what it's going to feel like to make that transformational choice to step away from what you know and to choose what you deeply desire.

During the COVID-19 pandemic, I decided to quit my job. It wasn't what many would have considered smart at the time, but I took a leap of faith—a leap that required a significant amount of reflection and courage. I tried to make excuses to stay, and I rationalized that my feelings of anxiety and disconnect were just a result of the pandemic, that they would pass and that everything would be okay. The problem, though, was that I was no longer fulfilled. I was working incessantly hard for someone else's vision, a vision I no longer felt connected to, and it was draining me. The meaning behind the work was waning, and I had lost my connection to myself while trying to force it.

For a long while, I internalized the belief that I was just a typical millennial who was entitled and didn't understand hard work. Millennials are often painted with a smugness or arrogance. We have a reputation for believing that we should just be handed that big project, that promotion or raise. I didn't believe I was entitled to anything. I believed that you had to work hard, and I did, but I also wanted to like the work I was doing. I wanted to enjoy where I spent half of my waking hours. Millennials are known for wanting to feel connected to their work and to do work that matters, and I 100% fall into that category. The beautiful part was that I did have a job I loved…at one time. But that changed—*I* changed. I had to not only recognize that I had changed, but also accept that it was *okay* that I had changed. What was once fulfilling no longer was. Unfortunately, society doesn't support these changes to our values, or this belief in valuing work that matters. Instead, the world around us makes us feel guilty for wanting to have an impact or wanting to feel fulfilled. Why, though? Shouldn't we all be encouraged to make the world a better place and to pursue fulfillment? Unfortunately, we're not taught that that matters; that's why it's so hard to pursue it. So instead of feeling empowered, I felt guilty, guilty for wanting to love what I was doing. I didn't believe I was worthy of having a job and a life I truly desired—and it didn't feel like I was allowed to have those things, either. Instead, I was forced to believe that I should just be grateful for what I had.

Let me set the stage for where I was before I quit my job and before I started the challenging process that led to this decision.

I was working in the non-profit sector, where I had grown from an inexperienced coordinator to a manager to having a seat on the leadership team of a small foundation, all within four years. I was, by societal standards, in a great position. I had a strong benefits package, a killer salary, and was being groomed to be the next CEO. On paper, the job was perfect, but I was burning out. I was continuously stressed and overwhelmed. I desired new opportunities to create and explore avenues to have a larger impact, but my role was already too big and I didn't have the time. When I expressed this to people outside my office, I was either told to pay my dues, work longer hours, or just be thankful I had a job (we were about eight months into the pandemic at this point). I was told I just had to work harder to gain that creative freedom.

I was never really fond of that belief system though —hustling and grinding to get ahead. Get ahead to where? And at what expense? What about what *I* wanted? Society trains us to believe that what we want doesn't matter, or that it simply doesn't matter *enough*. You can dream your little dream or have your desires, but at the end of the day, you have to get realistic. A job is a job, and you're not always gonna like it. This mentality is bullshit though, and just a conditioned belief. What if we decided the opposite was possible? What if we could have fulfilling jobs with meaning, creative freedom, and financial security, without the stress, agony, and burnout we're told to accept?

Trying to tap into my creativity outside of work, I started blogging at the beginning of the pandemic. I wanted to spread positivity in times of uncertainty. It was also helpful for me to flush out and process WTF I was feeling during those turbulent times. I had always enjoyed writing—I had even written a travel blog when I went to Southeast Asia after university. But being a writer wasn't considered a realistic dream, and it wasn't a job that could support me—or so my conditioned beliefs told me. It was a hobby at best. Well, the unrealistic dream of being a writer found a voice. It may have been a tiny one, but slowly I began to consider that that dream could play a bigger role in my life.

Over the course of the pandemic, I kept posting my inspirational blog posts. I told myself often that if I reached just one person, it was worth it, and it was those reminders that fuelled my desire to continue writing. They allowed that whisper telling me that I could choose what *I* wanted to gain strength, telling me that how I felt mattered. I considered that maybe I was no longer where I was supposed to be. I became more aware of my lack of fulfillment at work as I found fulfillment in writing and other areas. It was easier to see how disconnected I was when I started to feel connected elsewhere. And it was something as simple as writing a blog that helped me realize this.

My blog also reminded me what it felt like to do something I cared about. It helped reveal that my "perfect job" wasn't so perfect for me anymore. I wanted a role that had meaning to me. This caused internal turmoil for me when I realized that, despite the perceived success and opportunities I had at my job, it was no longer what I wanted. Before I could choose a new path, I had to walk through some deep emotions and confront deeper beliefs in order to make a change with confidence and certainty.

Choosing to quit my job in the middle of a pandemic when unemployment rates had skyrocketed wasn't what most would call "smart," and many people told me to wait. Well, ever since I've been able to walk, I've never been a big fan of being told what to do (it's true, you can ask my mama!). As I grew up and pretended I was an adult (yes, "pretended," because adulting is hard, you guys!), I often felt like I was on a different path than the others around me. I guess I never strayed drastically from the norm, but something inside me still nagged to go against the grain even a tiny bit. I still went to university, travelled before getting my first big-girl job, and moved into my own apartment in the city. Pretty standard, pretty typical. But when I was faced with the decision between quitting my job and choosing a life I wanted and staying and sucking it up, I chose to be different. I chose to do it my way and not do what everyone else told me to do.

The thing was, I wasn't prepared for how hard it would feel to make this decision. It meant I had to choose myself over all else. That's what quitting my job meant—believing that I was worthy of being chosen. It was difficult to choose what I wanted deep down and to stop living the life that made sense on paper. I had to listen to my inner voice that said I wasn't where I was supposed to be anymore. It meant giving up what I knew in favour of a life I could barely envision in my mind. But I knew I desired it. I trusted the whisper that told me that I was meant for something different.

I want you to know what it felt like for me to choose fulfillment and stray from the norm. The pages that follow don't portray inevitable success, but a rather agonizing process. Despite the agony, it was a process that was more than worth it. Through it, I gained the courage to choose fulfillment—and to choose *me!* This entire experience brought me a deeper learning and a deeper connection to my entire being. It was a battle within myself that I had never confronted before, not at this depth. But it brought me back to *me*, where I felt more aligned than I had in years.

When you embark on a similar journey and stray from the norm, you will also battle with your choices, and you might not win the first time—or the second, or the third. It will take time to believe that you are worthy and that you are strong enough to change your life. I don't want to lie to you and say it's going to be easy, but rather I want to be honest with you that change is hard. Transformational change is not an easy feat; it's something that will require you to show up in new ways. It will challenge you to admit what's not working. It will make you confront deep fears and beliefs about who you are. It will cause you to look at your life and reflect—is this what you envisioned for your life? Have you strayed from who you are or who you truly want to be? It's okay if you've drifted; you're not alone in this feeling. Only you can choose the life that brings you purpose and fulfillment though, and only you have the power to listen to that whisper guiding you. It's about time to start listening, don't ya think? It's time to act, because we only get one life, and it's your responsibility to get out there and live yours. Why are you waiting to choose the life you were meant to live?

As we walk through life, we're always going to be

confronted with new changes, questions, and decisions. We shift and change as we move through these things, and it's important to recognize when these changes happen. Things that once brought you joy and contentment might now cause stress and detachment. You might have achieved fulfillment at some point in your past but no longer feel that way. That *can* happen, and that is what happened in my job. Things changed, and it was scary to acknowledge that. So it's important to notice where you've changed and *when* you've changed, too. Acknowledge these changes and stop trying to force yourself to stay in a life that no longer suits you. Stop living the same chapter of your life over and over again.

I'm going to take you through my journey to choosing fulfillment and show you how my experience can prepare you to choose it too. To make it easy, I've created a seven-step framework for seeking fulfillment in your own life and understanding the emotions you will navigate during the decision-making process. It's like an instruction manual littered with my personal experiences. I will share my emotional highs and lows, the action steps I took, and the reflection practices I used to navigate the difficult choice to leave my job. These steps will help guide you when you're ready to take that transformational leap. That leap doesn't have to be quitting your job like I did; it could be investing your entire savings to go back to school, finally filing for divorce, or selling all your stuff to move across the country. The scenarios really are endless; what remains the same is the transformational impact choosing change can have on your life.

I'm sharing my story so you'll be able to prepare yourself for any big decision you might encounter when choosing the life you want. Our choices don't always make sense to everyone else, but as you follow along, you will come to understand that your choices only have to make sense to you. I was able to make big changes in my life with confidence, but only after I walked through the hard stuff.

What's to Come

Once we dive into the framework chapters, I will be sharing some of the practices I used that helped bring me clarity on my journey. You're going to find all of this and more in the Choosing Fulfillment Guide (which you already downloaded, right?). As a reminder, in the guide, you'll find journal prompts, awareness techniques and Spotify playlists you can vibe to! I created this guide as an extension of the book so you can work on these exercises whenever you want too.

When you use it doesn't matter, but using it will help you better understand your experience, thoughts, and emotions. We can't get results without doing the work—and I know you want results.

So if you haven't already, go download your *free* Choosing Fulfillment Guide:

www.theattitudeisgratitude.ca/yourguide

Now, if you haven't felt excited or content in your

life for some time, it's time to change that. Let's start to craft deeper meaning in your life, reconnect with who you really are, and put fulfillment back on your priority list. It shouldn't take a rock-bottom crisis to propel you forward. C'mon already! It's time for you to start living for you and choose the life you want. You already have the power, the courage, and the purpose inside you; it's time to tap into it. Stop waiting.

These pages are here to help prepare you for some of the turmoil you might feel when leaving behind your old life or an old version of who you were. But don't worry—on the other side of this is a life where you are choosing you. It's a place where your desires are possible, and it's freaking glorious!

I want you to know that you're going to need to be brave. It takes courage to choose yourself. Prepare yourself to do things that scare you and look fear in the face and say, "I see you, but I don't choose you." Choosing yourself will bring you face-to-face with your biggest fears and insecurities. We are programmed to talk ourselves out of extraordinary lives and to accept what we have and be grateful. We think, *Who am I to want more?* I say, "Who are you not?" Choosing an extraordinary life will require you to step outside of the well-defined box society has put you in. It requires colouring outside the lines and exploring your purpose. This will help lead you to a life you actually want to wake up to each morning, not one that you feel stuck living.

Shifting out of the life you are used to and into a life you want will require an active choice, intention, and deep self-reflection. Remember, fulfillment isn't found on the surface; it's found on a deeper level. You will be confronted by a mountain of things that try to block you on your path toward fulfillment. Your ego will try to keep you in the safe and comfortable life you know. That's okay; we just have to make that inner whisper stronger and louder than that dang ego of yours. You'll also have to turn down the volume of those around you, those who don't understand your desire for deeper meaning and purpose. This might mean going against what others think you should do. You will fight your own gremlins when you explore the idea of choosing yourself and your dreams. Doubt and fear will creep in, telling you to accept your life as it is, but what if you chose differently? What if you chose fulfillment over all else?

I'm here to tell you that you can. You no longer have to stay on the path someone else has chosen for you. You deserve extraordinary, and I believe—no, I *know*—you have a nudge on your heart that needs following. How many ideas, dreams, or wishes have you wholeheartedly wanted to come true but gave up because you didn't believe they were possible? Too often we leave our dreams tucked away in our hearts and minds, too afraid to let them out. We don't even give them a fighting chance. Our sense of worthiness holds us back, we put others before ourselves, and we don't believe in ourselves enough. We give up before even starting. We are afraid of betting on ourselves, so we diminish our dreams to dust and tell ourselves they're not possible.

That's where we go wrong. We fail to believe in the magical possibilities of a life we want and instead live lives that society tells us to. We accept the ordinary and keep to the status quo, but I think it's time to believe in the *extra*ordinary potential of our true selves. Don't you?

Choosing to quit my job was a tough decision to make. It wasn't logical, it was emotional. I've broken down my experience of choosing fulfillment into seven steps. These steps can apply to any major decision that you might be considering that has the power to change the trajectory of your life. While mine was quitting my job, yours might be moving across the country, ending that long-term relationship, starting that non-profit you've always dreamed of, or having a baby on your own. By sharing my experience, I want to encourage you to see the possibilities and give you the courage to choose that calling on your heart. It can be scary to choose yourself and to choose your dreams. It takes both faith and courage. The pages that follow will show you what to expect when you're trying to decide between the life you know and the life you truly want.

If you know me personally, you know that I'm pretty dang organized, so when reflecting on the best way to share my experience I thought I would break it down step-by-step—seven, to be exact. These seven steps—the catalyst, doubt, a need for space, fear, acceptance, guilt, and the act of living into fulfillment—are part of almost every journey to fulfillment. This seven-step framework will help you acknowledge your feelings as you live them and guide you forward on your own path. Before I begin to unpack these steps, though, I share a little more about what fulfillment means in Chapter 4 and share how these steps might relate to your personal story. The seven steps begin in Chapter 5, where I introduce what I call *the catalyst*, a trigger, an intense emotion, or a circumstance that sparks a chain reaction and causes you to question your current circumstance. It's a moment that will make you think, *Something has to change. This sucks.*

Chapter 6 will outline the battle within your self and the internal question, *Am I worth choosing?* Doubt causes us to question our worthiness and our belief that our dreams matter enough to be chosen, that our dreams *are* in fact realistic. It is in overcoming doubt that we can begin to step toward fulfillment and believe we are worthy of what we desire.

Chapter 7 will encourage you to find some separation, to step away from the ordinary day-to-day you are accustomed to. A change in your physical environment will help bring new perspective and reset the patterns you're used to.

Fear was the most challenging and longest stage of this experience for me, and I outline it in Chapter 8.

You will not only battle with your own fears, but with the projected fears of others. This stage caused me to look deep within myself and confront some of my biggest insecurities. Fear is hard to overcome because when we choose fulfillment it doesn't always appear logical and it won't always appear safe. It is in overcoming your fear that something shifts internally, where it all begins to feel possible.

Chapter 9 is about the blissful moment of acceptance, the point where you finally embrace a new vision for your future. It was during this step amidst the turmoil that I finally felt a sense of calm. I knew that I had to follow my heart and there was no turning back.

To round out the hard stuff, it's likely you will find yourself in a state of guilt. In Chapter 10, I share my struggles with letting others down. What I can tell you right now is that it's not a matter of *if* you let someone down, but *who* you will let down. The choice will be between you or other people, and it's time to put yourself first.

Chapter 11 describes that feeling when you finally let yourself fly. It's that feeling after you've made the decision, after it all becomes real, and you realize you did it, you chose yourself. And what a beautiful thing that is. It is such a wonder to know that your desires are a choice—a choice you can make right now.

These pages reflect my lived experience, but I hope you find yourself in my story as well, because we are all guilty of talking ourselves out of our dreams. Your journey will be unique to you though, so you might experience these steps in a different order, or maybe you'll repeat one over and over. This is why they call it a journey. You will learn things about yourself that you didn't know before, and this will challenge you to reflect and dig into who you really are. Without confronting our own gremlins and doubts, we won't have the strength to not only believe we deserve a fulfilling life, but to choose it as well.

It's scary to make a move from the known to the unknown. It's common to continue telling yourself to accept your life as is and to be grateful. You can choose this route, and you may even find some semblance of happiness, but it will be nothing compared to the life you could have if you mustered up the courage to follow that whisper on your heart.

Don't kid yourself either and try to half-ass your way to fulfillment. It's something you're going to have to choose and be ready to choose in full. There is no half-in. You can't think, *Well, I kind of want it,* or, *That would be nice*. You can't trick yourself into wanting more, because once you begin your journey and begin walking these steps, you won't make it past the first one. I'm here to help prepare you, but you have to be ready yourself. I know you know there is more out there for you, and I know you have a vision of a different life, a more fulfilling one. Anchor yourself in those desires. They will help you when it feels hard on your journey. With every step you take, you are on your way to fulfillment.

I walked through each one of these steps because I wanted to give myself a chance at an extraordinary life. I did the work, I asked the questions, I felt the feels, and I gained the insight that you can now take advantage of to take your life to the next level. These steps will help you to choose a life full of fulfillment in all areas. You can have it all. Now let's give you the framework you need to choose it.

My goal is not to get you to follow your dreams, but to wholeheartedly *choose them!*

What Does Fulfillment Really Mean?

You probably have some idea about what needs to change or what you want to bring into your life —but what if you want to change in multiple parts of your life? Our lives are complex, so it's defs possible that you might feel out of sync in more than one area. Maybe just one thing feels off, or maybe your whole life feels blah. Either is possible. For example, you could have the best marriage or partnership out there but have a job that drains you on the daily. Or maybe you're making tons of money but have no one to share it with, leaving you feeling alone and empty. Perhaps you are a recognized leader in your field but struggle with an eating disorder when you go home at night. It's possible to be fulfilled in one area and not in another, but is that really the end goal, to only feel good some of the time? I don't think so.

I used to put on different masks depending on what situation I was in. I would identify as Social Sara, Work Sara, or Relationship Sara, and I would show up as a different version of myself depending on the situation.

Eventually I learned I couldn't compartmentalize my identity. Each version of me was me, but I had to start seeing myself as a whole. It's similar with fulfillment. We might be feeling good in our business but feeling disconnected from ourselves, or we might have a kick-ass relationship while our health is in the pits. What I'm trying to say is that you can't compartmentalize fulfillment because you can't compartmentalize your life. Everything interconnects and flows in and out of everything else. So we want to take stock of how our lives feel as a whole and then decipher where we feel good and where we are feeling *blah*.

To get the shiny gold star, we want to seek and choose fulfillment in all areas of our lives. We want to feel fulfillment in our entire beings! The caveat is that there is no finish line when pursuing fulfillment; it's a journey that requires us to continually show up and continually choose it.

Depending on where you're at in life, this might feel a bit overwhelming if multiple areas of your life need some TLC. It might feel like there is a tonne of work to do. Breathe. It's okay—we are getting started right now, together. Right? Begin this journey with self-compassion and an understanding that it can take time. As you embark on your journey, you will need to be kind to yourself while also taking a hard look at your life. It will be up to you to want more, receive more, and finally to choose more. So, if you're feeling off in multiple areas, I encourage you to shift your focus to one area to start. Choose the area that feels easiest to address—start small and then go bigger! Change is a momentum game, so begin where you can make simple shifts to feel more uplifted and at ease. If you just have one area in which you want to feel better, *ah*-mazing. Let's get it!

Over and over again, I've tried to split my attention into different buckets and they all end up being underwhelmingly half-full, so I stress the importance of focusing on one thing. Focus on one area where you want to feel fulfilled first!

Here's a quick analogy. Imagine you have three piggy banks—you know, the cute ones with polka dots. Each time you have a little spare change or an extra dollar, you divide it between the three piggy banks. When all three are full, you get to treat yourself, say, with a relaxation massage or a new pair of jeans. Doesn't matter what it is. But how long do you think it's going to take to fill up those piggies when you divide your spare change between them? Instead, what if you plunked your coins into the same piggy every day? How much faster are you going to get what you want? The same applies to fulfillment. We need to focus our energy.

What's also important is being intentional. Fulfillment requires your active participation, which is why so many of us are lacking it. We are living outside of ourselves, out of sync, and out of alignment because we stopped focusing on what we want or we accepted that what we have is all there is. Do you want to continue living life on autopilot? Doubtful, because if you did, why would you have picked up this book? The challenge comes in changing your life as you know it. *Aaaaand* to change that is likely going to feel a bit scary. Which is exactly what the following pages dive into—how scary it can feel to shake up your life and change the life you have into the life you want.

You might be wondering, *But wait! I thought fulfillment was a good thing? Why would I be scared of it?* I probably would have asked the same question a couple years ago, but what I've learned is that so many of us have been lost and disconnected from who we are without even realizing it. In order to get back to ourselves, we have to begin asking ourselves what we want and start choosing it. This feels foreign and selfish at first because we're not used to it. To embody fulfillment at that deeper level will require bigger changes and reflection on your life as it is now. That's why it will feel scary. It will challenge you to change your life and step away from what you are used to.

Fulfillment is also not something you check off your bucket list and say, "Yep I achieved fulfillment, now let's go skydiving!" It's not like that. It requires you to remain intentional and continue choosing what you want. Someone has probably said to you, "Well, you don't always get what you want." Not with that attitude you won't! Of course, we won't get *everything*, but when you're aligned you won't need everything—you will simply need what is perfect and enough for you.

That brings me to my next point. Fulfillment is not one-size-fits-all. Who else rolls their eyes when they see that on a clothing tag? I mean, c'mon, these hips do not lie, and they will *not* be fitting into that one-piece! The same goes for fulfillment—it's not going to be the same for everyone. It is going to be 100% unique to you. You will need to stop pretending that you're the same as everyone else. You're not! You are special, unique, and brilliant! When you live into those elements that make you *you*, fulfillment will come naturally. The struggle is that we are conditioned to fit the mould and to be the same—because it's encouraged and it's accepted. Everyone is comfortable when things are the same. Well, I'm here to tell you that it's not your job to make everyone else comfortable. It's your job to live *your* life and to strive for the most fulfilling version of that life.

My story focuses on the decision to leave my job. If that isn't your situation, you might think, *Okay, how will this relate to me?* What's important for you to take out of the coming chapters is not the details of my experience but what it felt like for me to make this transformational decision. The steps I cover next can relate to any big life choice that feels hard. You've made difficult decisions before, but I can bet you've never sat down and made sense of it all. You've never taken the time to understand all the feelings that come up or why. I did.

By understanding what you might experience on your way to fulfillment, it will give you greater confidence when you enter the arena of decision-making. It won't look the same for you as it did for me, and your journey toward fulfillment won't be exactly the same either, but there will be parallels, and I hope you will see yourself in the pages to come. With that out of the way, are you ready to get started? We begin with the first step: the catalyst.

The Catalyst

As we live our lives, it's pretty common to go about our days according to a plan we envisioned years prior without even asking if it's what we still want. We forget to check in with ourselves and our days become monotonous and the same. They might even begin to feel unfulfilling, and that's when shit can take a turn. We forget that life is supposed to have a spark and forget the things that actually bring us joy.

At the early onset of the COVID-19 pandemic, I did an exercise to try to remind myself of the things that made me happy and made me feel like me. I created a High Vibe List, a practice that encourages you to list at least ten things that bring you joy or help you shift into a high-vibe state! This was important because, at the time, everything else in the world was getting turned upside down due to the pandemic. When I sat down to make this list, I honestly struggled with it. I thought joy had to come from big-picture things—a beach vacation, a promotion at work, a big house or yard, that fairy-tale kind of love. Things I couldn't access in the moment. I also thought about friends and family and those I loved. But where I really nailed it was when I realized joy came in the simplest packages. My first sip of coffee in the morning, blaring party jams in the bathroom while I got ready, soaking in a hot bath, sunsets and sunrises, and rockin' a snapback hat.

It's really the simple things that can shift our day-to-day experiences. I forgot this and stopped prioritizing joy as I got caught up in my job. I struggled to take a break, rest, or schedule a day off, even when people would tell me to. I felt like I couldn't. This is what begins to happen when we forget that joy and fulfillment are meant to be a part of our everyday existence. We begin to feel trapped in our own lives, and it feels hard to change them and even harder to think that something else is an option.

I was in an overwhelmed space, and it required a special kind of intensity and awareness to open my eyes and help me realize that the life I was living was no longer the life I wanted. I wanted joy and fun and to have the energy to live! No job was worth losing that. And neither is hanging on to that crappy relationship, that failing business, or that mortgage that leaves you house poor. If you're losing yourself by hanging on to something, something's not right. And it might take a particular circumstance for you to see things more clearly, to see that you do want more. What could this look like? It could happen when your debit card gets declined trying to buy a snack for your kid or when you wake up with a hole in your memory and a stranger in your bed. Perhaps your ongoing anxiety finally leads to a full-blown anxiety attack. It could be seeing that number on the scale that's the highest or lowest number you've seen in a long time. It could be any number of things, but what's key is that it shifts something inside of you. It pushes you to realize something's gotta give. Remember, this isn't rock bottom—rock bottom is far worse and hurts a helluva lot more. I don't want you to wait until it gets that bad. Listen to these experiences; don't make excuses or push it down. Listen when shit gets intense.

Maybe you haven't felt a shake-up and intensity of emotions just yet. Does that mean you're not on your path to transformational change? Not at all. You can always create change for the better in your life. Nothing is stopping you but you. What the catalyst represents is a deeper level of awareness, something you can't unsee. The catalyst marks a shift in one's mindset. A shift away from the blind acceptance of life as is, to a new awareness that there is more to it. The catalyst is a trigger that pushes you to realize you want more, or that something has to change. And I want to remind you right now that you have the power inside you to choose something else, that you're not stuck. You can choose to change your life right now.

> **"**
>
> *Getting through the days in this state is hard ... all I want is for the day to be over. I have no concept of time, yet I'm wishing for time to pass faster.*
>
> **"**

This is a direct excerpt from my journal that marked the onset of my catalyst, the time where my work struggle was gettin' real. My current position and how I was performing it were unsustainable. As much as I tried to hold on to it, it was draining me of my spark. I couldn't keep it going, nor did I want to have to try so hard. I felt like it should come naturally and joyfully, like it always had. I felt empty and overwhelmed by everything. I felt lost and high-strung and nothing like my normal self. It was in this state that my mind started a little dance and I began thinking, *Maybe I don't have to live like this. Is there another option?* Eventually, I had the lightbulb moment where I realized I had the power to choose differently. I also realized that, by not choosing to change, I was choosing to stay in my draining circumstance. The power was mine if I wanted it, and so I considered *the possibility* of quitting.

When I began to become aware of this strain on my day-to-day, I really started to question what I was doing. These subdued, drained, and overwhelmed feelings weren't like me. It was super weird for them to last for long periods and to reach me at my core. These feelings weren't those of just a tough day or a stressful project; these tapped into my foundational well-being. That hadn't happened before. I had always managed to juggle a long list of responsibilities—in fact, doing *all* the things was my MO. The year before the pandemic, I had the same full-time job, was enrolled in online classes and a member of a social change program, was volunteering on a board, and still found time to see my friends and stitch together a social life. If my calendar wasn't jam-packed with 100 things, something was off.

But this time I wasn't thriving in my busyness. I was fading, and fading fast. It was at this point that I had to question why I had no energy left at the end of the day. I had to ask if I still wanted to keep doing what I was doing and if I was willing to tough it out, work it out, or do something different. I realized that my job was no longer serving me and that I didn't want to tough it out. I wanted something different.

For many years, I had a deep appreciation for my role. In fact, for the first four-ish years, I loved my job and everything about it. I was even excited to return to work after vacations! This changed though, as everything in life can, and as I fell out of alignment I was no longer fulfilled by my job or by the work I was doing. My hope for you is that you can realize when something in your life that once brought you joy no longer does. That you can recognize when positive feelings no longer outweigh the hard ones. It's possible that something that once made you happy no longer does. Things can change and that's okay, but it takes awareness to understand that. Has something changed in your life?

New projects, events, and programs that normally would have excited me now stressed me out. At the same time, due to the pandemic, our work became more relevant than ever, giving my job more meaning. The organization I worked for help build parks and green spaces. Parks, one of the only public spaces that weren't taken away from us during the pandemic, became undeniably important. Our work had impact! Yet I felt more disconnected than ever.

We launched new response programs to meet the changing needs of communities, and instead of focusing on the impact they would have, I was focusing on the work it would take (take me, more specifically) to get them off the ground. That impact and meaning I was looking for as a millennial was there, but it wasn't the impact I felt connected to, and that mattered. As a result, my work piled up and my energy went down.

Because this disconnect and decline took place in late 2020, around the second wave of the COVID-19 pandemic, I thought my feelings were just a response to the stress of our changing world. I thought I needed to adjust and find a way to get through it. We were all dealing with uncertainty and confusion. But my disconnect, feelings of overwhelm, and lack of fulfillment went way deeper than the pandemic.

Approximately six months prior to the intensification of these feelings, I had already considered—well, "playfully dreamed about" is more accurate—the idea of leaving my job. It was getting repetitive, it was stressful, and it wasn't giving me the jazzy feels as it once did. I had been there for five years, and they often say that's a good time to switch it up, so I thought, *Hmmm, what else might I do?* At around that time, I started working with a life coach as well. In the first month or two of working with her, we chatted about big dreams and what I would do if I knew I couldn't fail. I started thinking about the possibilities. It was fun, and a little awkward, too, because it felt illogical and unrealistic. I had been conditioned well by the outside world to be "realistic," so I didn't really believe any of the ideas I came up with were possible. I would need a plan and concrete steps before those dreams could come to fruition. That's how my brain worked! I'm sure many of you can relate because that's what we're taught—to be logical, realistic, and to always have a plan.

Well, I never did figure out a plan. Instead, I was pushed beyond what I was willing to accept for my life. The stress wasn't worth it anymore, and because I had started dreaming about new possibilities earlier, it was easier for me to consider something else. This was beneficial for me because, if I hadn't gotten curious before it got serious, logic would have held me back. It was helpful that I considered something else at a time when I wasn't overwhelmed, at a time where there were no stakes. You can start thinking of new possibilities for your life, too. It costs nothing to start dreaming about the potential life has to offer.

Over the course of the next four to six months, I began to decline, and the disconnect from my work and my self grew boldly. I was feeling more stressed by simple day-to-day tasks. This would not be unexpected given the reality of the world at the time, but it wasn't normal for me. I had always managed stress quite well and had never experienced these feelings in the past, despite large workloads. It was a gradual progression, so it was hard for me to recognize what was happening. I also found ways to distract myself from my inner turmoil, first with a relationship and then with a mask of positivity. I acted as if I was thriving. I even convinced myself that I was doing fine, but in reality… well, remember that episode of *Friends* where Ross was *cue high-pitched voice* "*Fiiiine*"? Yeah, that was me. I had friends ask if I was okay, and I kindly and politely denied their offers for support and kept on pretending I was "fine." And of course, we all know what it means when someone says that they are fine—they ain't fine! Eventually I reached a point where I couldn't pretend or lie to myself any longer.

> *I woke up in a complete state of anxiety . . . That is not a place to be, a place to live. No job is worth that state of being.*

That was how I felt—my job was taking its toll. Emails piled up, work kept coming, and new projects felt like they sprouted up on the daily. I wasn't coping well, and it worsened to the point where I just wanted it to stop for one minute so I could catch my breath. I kept trying my hardest to show up for the team and get the work done, but really all I wanted was to just withdraw and avoid it all. Unfortunately, that wasn't something I would allow myself to do. So I kept pushing and forcing a smile on my face for every dang Zoom meeting I attended. This pushed me to lose that spark that made me *me*. I wasn't being authentic—my deepest core value—and living outside our values for any stretch of time takes its toll! It impacted my sleep, my motivation, and my ability to do, well, anything. I felt like I was physically vibrating with anxiety on the daily.

There are two moments that I can vividly recall where my walls crumbled. The first came after a weekly staff call. During the pandemic, everyone was working from home, which gave me the space to keep it together on the screen, only to break down after. I walked away from this particular staff call with a tight-ness in my chest. There wasn't anything in particular that had been different or overly stressful, but I just felt defeated. And after the call, I closed my laptop, walked over to my couch, and broke down into uncontrollable sobs, that deep cry where your whole body shakes and you can't catch your breath. I wasn't okay. I was burning out.

The second moment where the other side of my wall crumbled came after a doctor's appointment. I had been struggling with my hip, where pain and discom-fort prevented me from running and working out. Running and physical movement had been my outlets for years. Running helped me move stuck or built-up energy—a.k.a. anxiety and stress. I lost this outlet at a crucial time and didn't know what was wrong with my body, causing more stress. Between this, my workload, and a variety of other life happenings, I was upset that I didn't know how to fix my body. I needed my outlet, and I needed to get back to running.

My first attempt to problem-solve was to see a phys-iotherapist. I didn't see much improvement, and honestly, I wasn't a big believer in their treatment plan. I was then recommended to a sports med doctor who could explore whether there was a more serious issue. This doc threw down the gauntlet. He told me I likely had a tear in my hip socket that might require surgery to repair. I needed a special kind of MRI called an arthrography to confirm if that was the case, and it would take over a year to receive one. With wait times in our health care system, I would then have to wait an additional six to eighteen months to receive surgery to fix said tear. What I heard was that it would be two to three years before I could run again. I was devastated. Running was my outlet—even walking was a major meditative practice for me—and I couldn't even do that for more than thirty minutes without discomfort. I left the doctor's office and didn't get more than a few steps outside the building before the ugly tears started streaming down my face. I started sobbing on a street bench in the middle of downtown.

I want you to understand that I didn't wake up one day and feel this way. It took ongoing stress, an unsustainable workload, misalignment within myself, and a pandemic to create the circumstances that caused my catalyst. The catalyst itself won't be felt gradually, but circumstances will accumulate over time that lead to it.

Over time, things might become gradually more difficult, wearing you down. Things that once felt easy will now feel difficult. For example, one fight with your partner won't cause you to break up (well, at least I hope not), but continuous fighting will wear you down. The constant worry, crying, and sleepless nights take their toll. Pretending gets harder each and every day. Before we know it, we hit a wall without realizing that that's where we're heading. The moment you hit that wall, that is your catalyst, the thing that wakes you up! Both my staff meeting meltdown and downtown sobfest were me hitting my wall. It took two crashes to wake me up. I always was a stubborn woman.

When the uncontrollable tears hit post-staff meeting, I was so sad—not sad for me, but sad because I realized I wasn't going to be able to keep showing up for the team feeling the way I was. And showing up was important to me! I brought the light so many needed during this time. Sobbing in the streets was my realization that I wasn't showing up for myself. If I wasn't taking care of me, I wasn't much use to anyone running on empty. These two moments were my catalysts. They marked the first stage of stepping toward a new life path, a path that I had to choose, a path toward the fulfillment I deserved.

These moments opened my eyes, and my desire for something better grew. I no longer wanted to feel so out of control and remain complacent in my life. This was the onset to the tough decisioning that would follow, where I went on to battle doubt, unpack fear, and shed guilt before I found the courage to take the leap to choose fulfillment—and myself.

Your catalyst could be very different from mine and could unravel a different set of emotions and circumstances. Either way, in order for any experience to be your catalyst, it will come in with an *intensity* that makes you pay attention. It will bring you to the edge, where you will say, "I'm over it!" It will push you to want more than the hard or crappy stuff you know.

It could be feelings of overwhelm and disconnection, like it was for me, or it could be intense anger and frustration. It could be a taste of adventure and exhilaration or a new appreciation for life after death or deep loss. Whatever form the catalyst takes, it will be unique to your experience and it will be the exact push needed for you to take that first step toward choosing a life you actually want and owning that dream on your heart. The catalyst marks a pivotal moment.

Remember, your catalyst doesn't have to be hitting rock bottom, either. It shouldn't take something extreme to make you decide to start living a life you actually like. Your catalyst only requires a certain level of intensity that forces you out of your comfort zone *just enough* to make you realize you want something more. The caveat: you have to listen. It might come at you in multiple waves, like mine did, or smack you right in the forehead. Just don't wait for the universe to hit you with a Dwayne "The Rock" Johnson smackdown before you start paying attention. Wake up before life gets too hard and acknowledge that your life and your dreams are worth choosing right now. You only live once, so let's get living.

Regardless of what you might want for your life, if any desire or dream nudges on your heart, tap in and listen. Listening to these nudges and allowing your catalyst to propel you forward will help you reach greater fulfillment. So let your dreams grow, and let yourself get curious about what else there is and what else could be if you had the courage to take that leap. Create some space in your mind, your heart, and your life for your desires to take shape and breathe their first breaths. Your true calling likely doesn't reside in your current life, and it's likely bigger than anything you can imagine.

Endless excuses will pop up to block you from listening and stop you from exploring a life that truly makes you happy. I felt like I had to have all the answers and come up with a plan for it all to make sense before I could choose differently. I was justifying. We all do it, but what I now know is that it's usually the illogical steps that bring the most satisfaction. I had to burst my own belief bubble that I should have it all figured out before taking a chance, and that was scary AF. If you had told me a year before I quit my job that I would leave it in the middle of a pandemic, I would have looked at you and thought you were off your rocker. I never would have believed it because it seemed like such a drastic and risky life choice—*like, who would do that?*

insert emoji with her hand up! This girl! I gathered the courage to choose me and began living my life on my terms with fulfillment at the core. And you can too! Fulfillment can be yours if you want it. A life with meaning and connection is possible. You simply have to choose it and be willing to walk through some intense steps to get there. Anything worth having is worth fighting for, especially when it comes to you and your life. Stop waiting for life to come to you. Be a participant in your own life and start showing up for yourself today. Don't give up before your journey even begins.

Battle of Doubt

What's the real purpose of doubt, anyway? It usually stems from feelings of uncertainty and shows up where we lack confidence. But really, it's just an internal state that doesn't truly serve us. Unfortunately, doubt gets ingrained in our minds and runs wild in our thoughts. In some ways, I think we've become conditioned to doubt anything that doesn't fit neatly into the boxes of our minds. We immediately dismiss anything that's out of the so-called "ordinary," and instead deem it as unlikely, awkward, or uncomfortable. Perhaps this is why so few people choose fulfillment. Has it become a state so far from the norm that we don't even consider it anymore?

This needs to change. More people need to start choosing what they want and believe, not doubt, that it's possible. It's sad to think that you might doubt that a life of fulfillment is possible for you. Because why can't it be? What if we rendered it possible instead of dismissing it outright? What if we let go of the myth that life has to be hard? What if we allowed ourselves to believe that we can move from the ordinary to the extraordinary just by making a choice? Don't dismiss the possibility of fulfillment because doubt holds you back. Let's find the possibilities to flip that script.

Once my catalyst struck, I had to address my fierce attachment to the thing that was causing my struggle: my work. I was incredibly resistant to letting it go. It had become a huge piece of my identity, and I sought ways to create barriers that would prevent me from leaving. I would say to myself on repeat, *No one else can do my job*, supporting my belief that I couldn't leave. I created a story that would keep me in the well-defined box I was in, a story that said I was irreplaceable.

And, in some ways, I *was* irreplaceable. We all are, because no one else can do what we do or show up the way we can. What we bring to the table, whether that be in work, relationships, family, or community, is unique to us. No one can do what we do like we can. I came to understand that no one could do my job like I could, but that didn't mean someone else couldn't come in and do it *differently*. I also understood that I couldn't bring my gifts to the table if I was running on empty.

I was still paralyzed by doubt, though. This was a role I had grown into as a leader, where I was first encouraged to believe in my abilities. Leaving felt like stepping away from this perceived successful version of myself, a version I was pretty damn proud of becoming. It was also a version I thought others valued and recognized. And I couldn't stop asking myself, *Who would I be if I left?*

These questions and thoughts marked the beginnings of my battle with doubt. I played them over and over in my head and they became the early excuses for why I didn't believe I could step away. Choosing a different path didn't "make sense," so I tried to convince myself to stay and power through. I tried to tell myself that the stress and feelings of overwhelm would pass—*just breathe through them.* They didn't pass.

For my type A's out there, you'll appreciate what I did next: I made a list—well, two lists—to help organize my thoughts. The first wasn't your typical pros and cons list, but instead, it was a list of all the reasons I couldn't quit and all the deep-rooted beliefs that went along with them. It was easy to come up with the reasons why I thought I couldn't leave. But there's a yin to every yang, and so I also made a list of all the reasons I *could* quit, too. This helped me see a new perspective and shed light on the other side of the story. I forced myself to see the possibilities, not just the limitations, and this helped shift my perspective away from doubt. You can find this exercise explained in more detail in the Choosing Fulfillment Guide.

During this exercise, I identified a tonne of reasons to stay at my job, and these fuelled my doubts. I wrote down things like:

- My team will resent me for leaving.

- I will lose the respect of the Board of Governors, a circle of influential business people.
- I will be a bad leader if I leave.
- I should be thankful I have a job.
- I can't leave at a time where there is a shit tonne of work to do.

In my attempt to balance my perspective, I sought out thoughts that supported me leaving. I came up with things like:

- I'll create an opportunity for someone else if I leave.
- If I am left empty at the end of the day, it's not worth it.
- Respect is earned; it does not get erased.
- It is my life, and I am the one who has to live it.
- MY DREAMS MATTER. (Yes, this one was written in capital letters.)

The above are not exhaustive lists of the things I wrote down, but they provide a glimpse into the yin/yang that played out for me. The key was that I found a way to entertain both possibilities and to reach for reasons I *could* choose something different. It is easy to come up with the reasons you *can't* do something—those are the thoughts already playing in your mind.

But those thoughts will only keep you playing small and discourage you from wanting more. It is much more challenging to reach for the reasons you *can* choose differently, and that's why it's way more important for you to search for these.

I found strength by identifying new narratives that supported me and my desire to seek fulfillment. This gave me my power back. The narratives that supported fulfillment helped me believe I was worth choosing because all the reasons I said I couldn't quit weren't the only way to view my situation. Identifying these new narratives also helped me believe that my world wouldn't fall apart if I stepped away. What ways can you view your life or your situation differently? What is the other side of the story?

When I was struggling with doubt, it was truly a battle within myself. Shifting my mindset was key. It came down to how I answered the important question, *Am I worth choosing?*

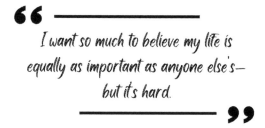

I want so much to believe my life is equally as important as anyone else's— but it's hard.

As you can see, I struggled with this question. Was I really worthy of being chosen? This question was heavy. I battled intensely with these thoughts and the responsibilities and expectations of everyone else—this will later tie to the chapter on fear. It felt selfish to choose myself.

The good news was that one of my personal mantras was (and still is), "*Selfish* is not a dirty word." Selfish is a word of love, a love for yourself. Selfish means you care enough about yourself and your needs that you deem them just as important as everyone else's. I had to get to a place where I was able to choose the belief that I deserved to feel good, happy, and fulfilled. It helped me realize that my life and how I felt in my day-to-day mattered. I didn't want to live stressed and overwhelmed anymore. I wanted nothing more than to be happy and free—but only I had the power to believe I was worthy of that life, and only I had the ability to choose that. If I didn't choose me, who else was going to?

It wasn't an easy narrative to change or an easy belief to adopt. So let me be the first person to tell you, *you matter*. Things will continuously pop up to make you doubt your worthiness again and again. And because you are used to being complacent and accepting the hard you know, you will get in your own way. But if you are going to move toward fulfillment, you, like me, will need to be able to answer "yes" to that question, *Am I worth choosing?*

Adopting the belief that you are worth choosing might take time, depending where you are in your journey. Our self-worth is a huge thing and requires nurturing every day. I believe I have stubborn confidence that says I don't have to do everything for everyone. I know I matter too. I've even been called selfish because of it, and it stung the first time I heard it. I've now come to wear it as a badge of honour, knowing I can put myself first. Not all of us are good at that though, and you might be one of the people who isn't. I want you to ask yourself, what is so wrong with putting yourself first? Why do other people matter more than you? It's simple: they don't. So try and be a little more selfish and believe you matter, too. Try to embody that feeling of worthiness and push doubt aside. I want you to gain the confidence to say, "*Yes*, I am worthy."

Despite the perspective shifts and new beliefs that I was worth choosing, I still wasn't convinced I could quit. After my major sob events, my main goal was to simply make it to Christmas break. Our office shut down between Christmas and New Year's, and I thought if I could just keep going until then, I'd be okay. I almost made it. Trying to use up my personal days before the end of the year, I scheduled a day off mid-week. That particular morning, I woke up feeling rested. The night prior, knowing I wouldn't be working the following day, I had been able to shut my brain off and get some freaking sleep. Usually I couldn't fall asleep because my mind would be buzzing and mentally scrolling the never-ending to-do list, so a good night's rest was a major win. Yes, at that time a good night's rest was a *win!* (And if you're thinking, *Wait, being tired AF isn't normal?* think again. You are meant to be rested.)

Back to that particular morning. I had slept in a little and was going to treat myself to some homemade pancakes, something special for my day off. I have loved pancakes since I was a little girl. I have fond memories of my grandma making little baby ones just for me. I was looking forward to a day of doing nothing, and I needed it desperately.

Unfortunately, my blissful morning was over before it even started. Shortly after I got out of bed, I received a text from my boss. She needed help with an application for one of the newer programs we had recently launched. I had built and administered the program, so naturally I was the go-to person. We were only a couple of days out from the Christmas break, so time was limited to get this application processed. I begrudgingly got on the phone and got to work on the application. It truly didn't take much effort to get the application done. In reality, it was a really easy request, but I was drained and frustrated. I just wanted this day off—and some dang pancakes! Was that too much for a girl to ask for? Of course, once I jumped on my computer, I got sucked into the email vortex, and three hours later I was still working. So yes, apparently that day, pancakes *were* too much to ask for.

During those few hours, my anxiety skyrocketed, and my mood hit a major low—I felt sad, empty, frustrated, annoyed, all of the shitty things. This reinforced my belief that no one else could do my job if they couldn't even file a simple application without me. As that day went on, every doubt about leaving returned with full strength.

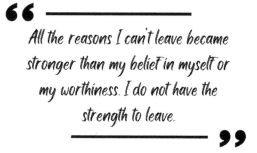

All the reasons I can't leave became stronger than my belief in myself or my worthiness. I do not have the strength to leave.

About two to three weeks prior to that day, I had had my post-staff-meeting meltdown. Remember when I curled up on my couch and cried so hard my whole body shook? Well, I had confided in a friend about that experience, and they were concerned about my mental health. It wasn't healthy to experience those kinds of extreme outbursts, and my friend encouraged me to go see my doctor. I resisted, but ultimately listened because I too was concerned that I wasn't going to be able to keep myself together on my own.

Long story short, I saw my doc and he prescribed

me anti-anxiety medication. I got the prescription filled the same day…and then it sat in my cupboard, not to be touched until a couple weeks later, when my boss made that simple request to process an application.

After I got off my computer that day, I was vibrating with anxiety for hours and I realized I wasn't able to calm myself down on my own. I allowed myself to admit that my anxiety was no longer in my control. That evening, I started taking the medication. Before that, I had been telling myself that I wanted to address the root cause of my anxiety on my own instead of masking it with a tiny pill. Up until that day, I had felt like I was strong enough to address what I was going through, or at least work toward figuring it out. I resisted, as my stubborn ass does. But that day, I hit a wall and I surrendered.

In hindsight, I should have listened to my gut. I didn't need the medication. I was on it for less than six weeks, barely long enough for any change to take place. What I really needed was to listen to my heart and to choose myself. Medication wasn't going to help me do that. What it actually did was cause me more anxiety as I tried to find the right drug, the right dose, and wait for it to start working. It never did. In some ways though, I do believe it provided a placebo effect that gave me renewed confidence and the strength to believe that I had the clarity to make this choice, to choose differently.

Quick note! I don't think taking medication is

wrong, nor is it shameful. I've known many people who have taken medications to help them over the years, and it *has* helped. Sometimes we need that extra boost and added support to regain control of ourselves. Once we get there though, we have to ask the hard questions. What is causing these feelings to begin with? It is our responsibility to address our own experiences, stress, and unhappiness, or we will continue to struggle with the same thing forever. No pill is going to change that.

I knew the cause of my anxiety was my job, and I knew deep down that it wasn't the pandemic, depression, or a by-product of social isolation (though it's possible those things accelerated it). I truly believed it was my job that was causing me angst and turmoil because it was no longer right for me. I was out of alignment, I was out of soul, and that's why I was struggling so deeply. Medication couldn't fix that; only being true to myself would bring me back to peace. I didn't know that at the time though, and so by making lists, confiding in a friend, and surrendering, I was able to keep moving forward. It didn't feel like it at the time, but each day, I took a tiny step, and I was getting closer to overcoming my deepest doubts.

Doubt can creep into your mind in big or small ways. It's like a weed—it spreads fast and the roots grow deep. That is why doubt is such a strong emotion. It is easy to give up your power when consumed by it. Doubt preys on any crack in your belief system and will have you questioning, "Am I enough? Can I do this?" Your catalyst will open your eyes, allowing you to see that the life you are living isn't the life you truly want. You know you don't want what *is* anymore, and you know there is a possibility of something different. Then doubt creeps in and weakens your belief that it's possible.

The battle with doubt is not an easy one to tackle. It requires you to look inward, and sometimes that is a messy process. It's likely going to feel pretty gross at times. At the end of the day, choosing yourself is a process, a process that has the power to bring you back into alignment. It is in alignment where you will find the path to come back to yourself.

It's going to be easy to find all the reasons not to do something, not to rock the boat, and to stick with the status quo. It requires intention to seek out the reasons why you *can* choose differently and make a change. Only in seeking answers that support your own fulfillment will you find them. Doubt is strong, but you are stronger.

Remember, there is a yin to every yang, a positive to every negative, and a reaction to every action. Any doubts that are preventing you from choosing a life you want have an opposing narrative. Write the other side of the story, the story that says, "I am worth choosing and I can have a fulfilling life on my terms." The story that gives you strength to step away from what is no longer serving you. Only you know when your life is no longer in alignment, and only you can choose a new path.

Doubt might pop up in various ways, or at a different time in your personal journey, so don't force yourself into a cloud of doubt if you're not feeling it. It will come up naturally when your decision grows in potential and possibility.

Each difficult experience is going to teach you more than the easy ones ever could. I wish the easy days and the good feels taught us the best lessons, but let's be honest, would we really learn anything if it felt good? So when doubt does creep up, remind yourself that there is a lesson in this for you; it's all part of the journey. And if you have somehow managed to sidestep feelings of doubt altogether, you have some kick-ass self-confidence, and I say, all the power to you! Keep going and don't look for ways to create doubt.

Your desire for a different life, a life that truly fills you up, matters. It matters just as much as everyone else's. It is up to you to not only believe you matter but to welcome that belief into your heart. That is the only way you will be able to take the steps necessary toward a life you choose. I believe in you, even if you don't just yet.

Take Some Dang Space

W hen our lives aren't a reflection of what we truly want, it can be helpful to step away to renew our perspective. When we're immersed in the same old same old, are we not going to have the same old same old thoughts and continue with the same old same old routines? Sometimes we need to switch up our space to switch up our mindset.

I've often heard that our physical environment is a direct reflection of our internal environment. This has proven true for me many times when I've looked around and seen clutter and dishes, and dust bunnies gathered in the corner. My mind often needs the same kind of sweep my surroundings do. It's amazing what simply cleaning up your physical space can do for your mind. This grows even more beneficial when you leave the confines of your regular four walls to surround yourself with new ones. Something as simple as visiting my parents' acreage can give my mind a refresh.

Our internal and physical environments are linked.

And when our physical and mental spaces intersect, we might need to remove ourselves from the environments that are no longer serving us. This can help us think differently and open our minds to new possibilities.

As I struggled with my decision to leave my job, I realized I needed space—from everything. After spending months working my tail off, hiding behind a mask of positivity, and swimming through my own pool of doubts, I was tired, physically and mentally. I just needed to stop. I needed to step away from my day-to-day work and shut down the emails *hard*. I needed to step away from social media and the ongoing pressure to be positive. I needed to step away from people. I didn't have the energy to show up for others; I needed to take some dang space and simply show up for myself.

And so, for about two to three days, I allowed myself to wallow, eat all of the food, and sleep as long as I wanted. And by "allowed," I mean I resisted it fully! It felt uncomfortable to let myself wallow. I heard that outside voice saying, "Suck it up, buttercup." Well, sometimes we've just gotta eat that buttercup instead and walla walla wallow. We can't just suck it up and force ourselves back into alignment. It just doesn't work that way. Whatever it is you're needing or perhaps struggling with, I am giving you permission to wallow in it. (Temporarily. This is a hall pass, not a season's pass.)

As much as I knew I needed this time to just be, I

really struggled with it. I wasn't used to giving myself this kind of space to do nothing. I had trained myself to work in overdrive and to always be doing *some*thing. In hindsight, it was obvious I needed this time more than I realized. My energy was stagnant, and I had no desire to do even the simplest things, like get out of bed. I felt heavy and dull. I had lost all semblance of a routine, and I wasn't taking good care of myself. Thank god drivers from Skip the Dishes were doing contactless delivery! I would have been so embarrassed if they knew it was me each time I ordered a bottomless pit of Chinese food. I was stuck, and I struggled to give myself permission to be there—but I needed to.

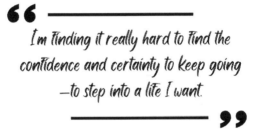

I'm finding it really hard to find the confidence and certainty to keep going —to step into a life I want.

It's important to recognize and let yourself feel everything you may be suppressing. My body was telling me to rest. For almost two weeks, the span of our Christmas break, I slept ten to thirteen hours each night because I was exhausted on all fronts. I required rest. You might need to cry for multiple hours, sleep, then cry some more. Perhaps anger is your outlet and you just need to scream and release all the suppressed words you've held in for so long. Or maybe you need to punch some shit. If that's the case, I encourage you to grab your least favourite pillow and go to town. Our bodies and emotions will tell us what we need, but we need to listen and then give ourselves permission to feel it and let it out. The key is *listening!*

To make things even heavier, I wasn't only struggling with work and this big decision, but also with deep personal fears that I would get stuck in this overwhelmed state. I was so afraid that, if I gave into these feelings wholeheartedly, I wouldn't be able to find my way out. It's intimidating to walk into your own darkness. Eventually (and reluctantly), I let that darkness in. I trusted I wouldn't be in the dark space forever. For months, every nook and cranny of my brain space was being utilized by work. I would wake up thinking about work, I would go to sleep thinking about work, I would even *dream* about work! And you can't undo that kind of mind race in a day. Slowly, I gave myself space, rest, and permission to stop resisting and to feel what I needed to feel. I surrendered little by little, which helped me regain my inner strength and personal perspective. A few days to myself was not enough to get me back to "normal," but it was enough to allow me to catch my breath. Three days to yourself might be all you need to tap back into yourself.

When everything feels hard, committing to a major life decision can feel impossible. Letting go of the familiar feelings of my life was hard to accept. It felt overwhelming to think about giving up what I knew, until I allowed my brain to simply calm TF down. Only then did I begin to process the possibility of leaving my job for real. Without creating that mind space, I wouldn't have been able to unpack this monumental life decision. Fear would have beaten me. The time I took to sleep for hours and check out from everyone and everything was necessary—and it helped!

Creating space is crucial to bringing clarity because by doing so, you allow yourself to process what you're feeling. When our days are filled with traffic jams, and to-do lists, and book clubs, and dishes, and partners, and family dinners, and, and, and, we have no dang space to listen to our own thoughts or figure out what we really need. We push down the ugly feelings or thoughts because we don't have time to deal with them. Taking the time and space allows you to let those feelings and experiences bubble up. We need the focused time to think, without distractions. If we're not willing to confront our darkness, our light won't be able to find its way in. You not only need time to process; you also need distance, physical space from your life as you know it. When you physically change your surroundings, it allows you to look at your life through an external lens. You're no longer in the thick of it but looking in from the outside. This allows you to be more objective. Take the space! You need the focused time.

You might not have the same opportunity I had to be a hermit for a few days, but I fiercely encourage you to find a way. Remember our yin/yang list, where we wrote down all the reasons we can and all the reasons we can't do something? Finding a way to take the space you need to reflect, release, or recharge might take the same kind of exercise. Here are some helpful questions to consider:

- Who can I rely on to help me out?
- Do I have vacation days left?
- Can I afford to go away by myself for the weekend?
- Can I stay at a friend's house?
- Can I talk to HR?
- Can I cancel that meeting and go home early?

Resist the knee-jerk "no" response you're likely going to feel when asking these questions. Try to find ways you *can* take the space and don't fixate on why you can't. You require that distance so you can start to make sense of what you're feeling. Create the space you need in doses as big or small as you need. And *do not apologize for it*. You are entitled to your healing and entitled to your space. Take those things without apology.

This physical and mental separation will help you navigate the rest of this process. It's necessary to give yourself that time away. You might need this space at a different time than I did, or perhaps it'll take more time or less time. Regardless of when you take this space, it's vital that you take it. I firmly believe you need to create distance from the thing/person/job that is no longer in alignment in your life. This will help bring clarity. If you are continuously and forever immersed in the same life, you make it easy to believe that's all there is. Don't get sucked back in. Create the distance necessary. It doesn't have to be long, but I would recommend at least three days of separation to start. And to clarify, this is not a girls' weekend away or a weekend filled with wine tours, shows, or other distractions. This time away is for you to be with yourself and sit with your thoughts. It's time needed to reflect on the life you have and ponder the kind of life you want. And okay, you can enjoy your favourite movies, order in that fatty take-out, and sleep as much as you want. But remember you are no longer here to accept your life as it is. You are here to choose fulfillment, remember? So when you take this time away, ensure you use it to reflect on your current life, to feel any emotions that come up, and to seek clarity on what you want to change.

Each day I delayed my decision, I was delaying my dreams and my life. Each day that *you* delay making a decision, you're delaying *your* dreams and *your* life. It's time to stop delaying! I had a decision to make, and so do you. I had to choose to leave my job or to stick it out and stay. Whatever decision I made, I had to embrace it and move forward. I had to make a choice because sitting in indecision was agonizing and uber unproductive. I wasn't serving anyone by being half-in on both sides, and neither are you. This is why I cannot stress enough that you need to take a step away. Be all-out for just a minute. I can promise you it will give you more strength and increased clarity before you confront what comes next: fear.

Overcoming Your Fear Stories

Fear is a story we tell ourselves about why we can't do something. But what about the story of why we *can*? We shouldn't so easily dismiss the perspective that we can have extraordinary, and accept what is without question. It doesn't make sense, but we're all guilty of doing it.

When it comes to the fight with fear, it's pretty unlikely that you're going to take one swing and land that knockout punch. You're going to have to keep throwing punches until your hand is raised at the end of it all. In fact, it's likely you're going to go the full five rounds before you are named victorious. It could be months, maybe even years, before you gain the courage to overpower your fear. I don't say that to make it sound burdensome or out of reach; I say that because our fears are deeply rooted, and it takes time to understand and overcome them. Everything happens in due time, so try not to get frustrated with fear or give up that dream of a fulfilling life. Instead, keep that vision alive in your heart and remind yourself that you have the power inside you to choose something different and better for you. No one can take the dream away from you *but* you. I know you have it in you to beat fear and anything that stands in your way. So don't be discouraged—get ready to fight.

What will help you get closer to choosing fulfillment is tackling your fears one by one. Over time, you'll be able to pinpoint the pivotal fears that are holding you back. Then comes the work to rewrite those stories. The work of rewriting these stories becomes vital when your vision for a different life doesn't align with what "they" think. Who the heck are "they" and when did we give them so much power over our lives?

I felt a deep resistance to changing the direction of my life, rooted in fear and supported by several stories I was telling myself. None of it seemed logical. It was through my fight with fear that I shifted from a place of uncertainty to a deeper knowing inside that this was the choice I had to make. Overcoming fear allowed me to level up into a braver and stronger version of myself.

People naturally project their fears onto others, most of the time unknowingly. They do it because they care; they think they are protecting us. I found a way to tune in and separate other people's fears from my own by focusing on my own fear stories first. We have all been moulded by society, our childhoods, relationships, and all the ups and downs that life has given us—and all of those experiences shape how we respond to our present situations. Your life experiences are unique to you, and therefore, how you respond to a situation is going to be different than how someone else might respond in the same situation.

So don't let someone else's fear choose for you, and stop following everyone else's advice!

Their advice is steeped in their own fears. We have enough of our own fears that we carry around that hold us back; we don't need to take on everyone else's too. It's essential to understand your own fear stories before spilling the beans about your desires over a glass of wine or two. Because once you start sharing your thoughts and plans with others, you *will* be hit by more fears to wade through. Don't say I didn't warn you...

Break down your own fears and build trust in yourself first. The exercise "identify your fear stories" in the Choosing Fulfillment Guide can help you do this.

I had a carousel in my mind packed with fears that were continuously spinning round and round with no slowing down. I played these stories over and over in my head, and these were only the ones that I was consciously aware of. Once I tackled the fears I knew, I became aware of deeper unconscious fears that I also had to overcome. Want to know some of the early stories I made up? They went something like this.

- *If I quit, I'll be irrelevant. No one is going to remember who I am, and my network will fall apart. If I am no longer Sara Stepa, Director of Programs, who am I?*

- *I'm going to look stupid. Who quits their job in the middle of a pandemic? Am I just going to quit without a plan? What am I going to do about money? No more paycheques—what about my bills? Can I still go out with my friends?*
- *Quitting means I'm a bad leader. If I can't keep it together, I'm not deserving of being in a leadership role.*
- *Am I even enough on my own? Without my title, the organization, the team, a mission, what purpose do I fulfill? Will I sleep until noon and binge eat snacks every day?*
- *Will I become isolated? I already live alone; is it smart to cut off the one constant form of interaction I have? Will I become depressed? Am I depressed?*

MY FEAR FLIP

What helped bring me closer to my decision was when I was able to flip my biggest fear. Once I reframed this fear, I took its power away. It allowed me to connect to my higher self and believe in both my potential and my ability to take the leap. This fear flip was pivotal! It helped me gain traction in overcoming all the other fears that were holding me back.

My biggest fear was believing that if I quit, it meant I wasn't strong enough.

Just the act of considering quitting my job made me feel like I was giving up. I fiercely held on to the identity of being a strong woman, one who could take care of herself. As a leader in my organization, I felt this deeply when it came to the team as well. If I left, I felt like I was abandoning my team, my boss, and the organization.

66

The reason [I thought] ... I was leaving was because I couldn't handle it. [I thought] I wasn't strong enough, but that's actually not true ...

99

I had to rewrite this fear story, replacing it with one that gave me strength.

66

I no longer want to work there because I'm not connected. I don't believe in the mission. It is impacting my happiness because I have nothing left at the end of the day. The reason I'm leaving is because it's my time to move on to new things for me, not because I can't handle it.

99

This new story came through to me because I wanted to believe it. My yin/yang list helped me realize there were two sides to every story. Journaling and writing down my thoughts also helped me shift from a mindset of failure to a space of possibility. More distance was growing between me and my role. I was no longer half-in but over half-out. The space I took allowed me to see these new perspectives.

By giving myself space, I had more clarity and mental capacity to fight through and create a new belief, one that would give me courage to move forward. I never would have been able to quit my job with the underlying feeling that I was giving up. By rewriting the strongest fear I knew, I was able to rewrite others. I held tight to the belief that this was the best thing for me. I wasn't a quitter, I wasn't giving up—*I was choosing myself*. I had a responsibility to choose myself and, by identifying my truth, I had more power and resilience to dissect other fears that came at me.

So I did. I began to uncover and tackle more of my fear stories I listed earlier about being on my own, not having a plan, missing out on that regular paycheque, and feeling needed and valued. I was able to ask how much external validation I needed to feel important and thought, *Are you enough for you, Sara?* This is a question you may need to ask yourself.

My battle with fear was convoluted and multi-layered and was far from straightforward. I couldn't approach this stage with a fixed mindset. This means I also can't give you a "how-to guide" to tackle your fears. You will be confronted with your own fears and deeper gremlins that will try to block you from choosing the life you want. And it's hard to overcome, but 100% possible!

I won't pretend that all I had to do was overcome one central fear and everything started to fall into place. I didn't shift out of fear by rewriting one story. I would move forward one day and retreat the next. There was a considerable amount of give and take, but I kept trying. I wasn't going to be able to achieve my dreams by staying in a job that sapped me of my energy; that was something I was sure of. I also knew that I didn't want to keep feeling the way I was. No one should live in a constant state of stress and overwhelm. I mean, what kind of life is that?!

Could I have tried to change my work environment? Yes, I could have tried, but once I realized I was no longer connected to the work, there was no coming back from that. I also allowed myself to desire more freedom and more opportunity to be creative. I needed time for that, time I didn't have in this role. And no matter what the organization would have done to help or support me, my heart just wasn't in it anymore, and I wasn't going to be able to forcibly change that. I started to internalize that it was time for me to move on.

As I gained more perspective about my fears and

more courage about the choice I was trying to make, I knew it was going to take a bold move. As my personal awareness grew, I began to feel more comfortable in my fear. I felt I was getting a handle on it—and then I was hit by my unconscious fears. *Arrrgh!* That was when I learned that our unconscious fears are revealed and mirrored back to us through the opinions of others.

This is an important point I want to get across. Your unconscious fears *will* pop up in other people's opinions. When you understand that people reflect your own fears back to you, it gives you more power in how you respond. When someone's words trigger you or a fear pops up again and again, this is telling you that this fear still lives inside of you. Remember those five rounds I mentioned at the beginning of the chapter—this is those rounds in action. You will be required to fight those fears over and over until you're able to break them down and overcome them for good.

Word of advice: Don't proclaim anything to the world until you are ready to own it within yourself. Other people's opinions have the power to distract us. We can be triggered by what they say, especially when their words and opinions touch on our insecurities. When their words don't cause a reaction, you can confidently dismiss or accept their perspective with kindness and move on ahead. You'll understand their fear as theirs and not your own. So when you flare up in defence or cower in response to someone's opinion, they have touched on a fear you have not yet addressed or overcome. This is the best way to be alerted to your unconscious fears. Pay attention to your response to the words and opinions of others. These little tests are guiding you toward greater awareness of your fears. This will happen more frequently as you open up and start telling people you're going to make a big change.

Before writing this, I thought my fears and the fears of others were completely separate from each other. But humans are funny creatures who like to stay comfortable. We will seek out information that validates our beliefs and the stories we tell ourselves. Whether these beliefs are serving us or holding us back doesn't matter; whatever we hold most true in our hearts will be reflected back to us. You will find reasons, people, and opinions to validate your fears and deter you from stepping in and levelling up. Once you've broken down your fears, you will no longer seek those opinions or be triggered by those thoughts shared by others. You'll be able to confidently and safely know, "This is their fear" and graciously pass it back.

When you are stepping into a new path or different circumstances, it is uncomfortable and you likely won't have many people around you showing you or telling you that it's possible. This makes it difficult to go against the grain. There is a lack of evidence that a new path will lead to success and fulfillment. There is no guarantee, and this is where our egos really get their panties in a bunch. They are not programmed to accept this kind of unknown. The ego prefers that you stay in the safe and comfortable spaces you know.

This is why I can't stress enough how important it is to get a handle on your internal environment before you look outside yourself. Our egos create enough chaos, so quiet your own gremlins first. Once you step outside yourself, you *will* find the validation that reinforces your beliefs—good or bad. In order to choose the life you want, I encourage you to spend time in your own head and spend time with your own fears before you ask others for their opinions. You want to feel ready to own the change you're seeking and feel like it's possible.

I heard many opinions from people, and I constantly felt I had to defend myself. At the end of the day though, other people's opinions didn't matter as much as my own. All I could control was how I felt, how I responded, and how I chose to live my life. I didn't know how people might react to my choice, but I couldn't afford to allow others to plant their opinions in my mind and for them to take precedence over my own. I had to ask myself, *Who are you making this decision for?* If I quit my job, I had to own and understand on a deeper level that I was making this choice for me. I had to live my life the way I wanted.

Now I'm not saying to cut everyone out of your decision-making process. You might have a phenomenal partner who can handle these conversations or a best friend who helps you navigate life's challenges, or perhaps you have a coach to guide you. You can lean on others, but just keep two things in mind. First, your fears are your fears and their fears are theirs; try not to get them mixed up. Get confident with your new stories. Second, make sure the people you confide in understand how special seeking a life of fulfillment is. You don't want anyone to kill your vibe. *cue Kendrick Lamar*

WHEN YOU START TO OPEN UP

Once I felt comfortable in my own fears, I gained enough confidence to start confiding in others. I started to tell people I was thinking, just *thinking*, about quitting my job. Once I started sharing, I was brought back to many of the same fears I thought I had already overcome. Remember, if we haven't truly overcome a fear, it will come back again and again. Fear doesn't follow a straight line.

I began telling my family and some of my close friends about my potential choice. Some weren't surprised at all—they knew I had been struggling at work—while others were concerned. These shared conversations held weight, and each and every one tested me.

Slowly, though, I was able to beat my fears, and I began to understand that people were simply trying to protect me from their own fears. Notice how I said *their* fears. I came to understand that their insights were coming from a place of what *they* would do in my situation, but it didn't have to be what I would do in mine.

One conversation acted as a turning point for me. I understood I was done, and I felt confident that I was going to quit, so I confided in a friend. This friend was also a past coworker who had left the same organization as me a couple years prior. I was fortunate to have someone who could relate so closely to my experience, but that didn't mean I wasn't still confronted with more fears—nor was she 100% on board.

I hadn't seen this friend in a while, but I was always stoked to reconnect and catch up. I had missed working with her a tonne after she left the foundation, but she had known she was ready for something different and ended up opening her own business. We started our catch-up date at her little tea shop and wandered down to the beautiful river pathways for our stroll.

After some basic chitchat, I opened up to her and shared that I was thinking of leaving the foundation. It was the first time I had talked about this decision with realness in my voice. Telling someone who I knew could relate helped me feel safe. She expressed surprise, but she also completely understood. She knew the team culture and understood the focus and impact of the foundation's work. And we shared a mutual feeling of wanting something different. I went on to explain how drained I felt in my role and that I just wasn't connected to the work anymore. It bothered me not to care as I once did.

As we continued to walk, she asked what I was going to do instead. What was my plan—surely I had thought about my next steps? *Eeek!* That's where I didn't have the answers. I had all the clarity in the world to explain why I wanted to leave, but none about what was next for me. This felt a little unsettling and because I didn't have answers to her questions, my friend was a tad cautious with the advice she offered. If I didn't know what I wanted to do next, the decision was riskier. *But was it?* Or are we simply programmed to need all the answers? We fear the unknown more than we fear change, and so even though my friend understood the stress and disconnect I was feeling with my job, it was still hard for her to wrap her head around this choice.

Despite her possible reservations, she still wanted to support me, and so we continued our river stroll with the icy river flowing next to us and shifted our convo to the possibilities of what I might do next. Did I want to stay in the non-profit sector? Was I going to explore the writing world? Would I start my own business? All of these felt like possibilities at the time, but I wasn't ready to choose. I had a pull toward writing, but I was far from being able to own that at the time. When I thought about next steps, it felt exciting and, I'll admit, a little intimidating. I was already trying to figure out one big step—now I had to plan out everything that came after, too?! No, I had to keep my focus on this one decision. I was never going to have all the answers about what came next, but I did need to make space for opportunities to come in.

As the time passed with my friend, I noticed that in spite of the presence of some unsettled feelings, I felt collected. As the conversation went on, I was feeling more and more confident about leaving. Internally, something began to shift. I felt like leaving my job was the right move. Even without all the answers, it still felt right in my heart (I still wasn't ready to act, though).

I truly believe the only reason our conversation took me in this direction instead of pushing me back into my fear zone was because I spent time with my fear first. I spent time in my own head and had answers for so many of the questions that came up. I felt calmer within before I sought out someone else's opinion. This is what I've been saying all along and it's what I encourage you to do as well. The conversation with my friend brought me another step closer to embracing and choosing fulfillment.

I was thankful I had this shift before I opened up to someone else whose opinion I really valued. My final fear test came from someone else, my best friend, my ride-or-die who believed in me wholeheartedly in the best ways she can. But she was intensely afraid for me to make this decision.

She knew I had been struggling with anxiety, and she was concerned that I was being hasty. Lacking motivation, feeling overwhelmed, having limited desire or energy to do things, and struggling with sleep can all be symptoms of depression and/or anxiety, and I was experiencing all of them. She felt the root issue was not my job but rather a mental health problem.

I didn't disagree with her that what I was feeling could lead to a mental health diagnosis, but I knew deep down that that wasn't it. I wasn't immune to her fears though, and I took into account what she said to me. I wondered if I was in the right mental state to be making this choice, and I was brought back to my fear that maybe I wasn't strong enough to make this choice.

This turned out to be just another fear story rearing its ugly head. It was then I had a realization…

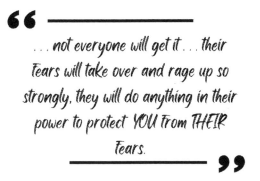

> … not everyone will get it … their fears will take over and rage up so strongly, they will do anything in their power to protect YOU from THEIR fears.

This friend had the best intentions and shared her concerns with pure love, but it was up to me to know if her concerns were valid in my situation. I had to disconnect her fears from my own and realize that this wasn't a decision she would have been comfortable making. The great thing was, she didn't have to. This was my choice, and I was the one who had to make it—just like you will be the one required to make yours.

Societal conditioning teaches us that others' needs and opinions are more important than our own and will cause us to fear choosing ourselves. This puts fear in the driver's seat, and we allow it to make our life decisions in favour of keeping everyone else comfortable. Changing that view and putting yourself back in control takes some dang courage, but you can do it. Once you regain your own power, you can choose to embrace who you are and the potential of who you can be. You get to choose the direction you want to go.

Fear is a protective response that exists to keep us safe and is necessary for our survival...yeah, yeah, yeah. What fear is really doing is just getting in the way of you and the rest of your joyful, extraordinary, and fulfilling life. Fear tricks you into thinking you need to have a guaranteed outcome. Well, I hate to break it to you, but nothing is guaranteed, and your life can change in a flash. Did we learn nothing from the pandemic?

When we step toward the lives we want, fear isn't going to disappear, so instead of trying to eliminate it, why not learn to sit with it? Invite it to hang out at your table and stop awkwardly avoiding it. Become friends with your fear. Your fear can be one of the best avenues to help you gain insight and clarity.

Fear is a strong emotion. It's meant to be, because it's hardwired in us to keep us safe, but keep in mind that most of the fears you're feeling are simply dreamed up in your own mind. They're not real physical threats you need to protect yourself from. They are based on past stories and protective behaviours you've built throughout your lifetime. And at the end of the day, most of what we fear is not to be feared at all.

You can break down your fears by asking more questions and playing out the worst-case scenarios. You can rewrite your fears and create new and supporting narratives. Go inside your head and heart first; this will lead you to a better understanding of your fears.

I weave the concept of your own fears and the fears of others together throughout this chapter. The core understanding you need to take from this step is that *your* fears are *your* focus. Other people's fears are just a by-product and something you will experience along the way. You can't control what they might think or feel, so don't spend your precious time trying to convince them. You can hold space for their insecurities, but it's not your job to change their mind. When it comes to the fear stage, your own fears are all you can control.

Fear is one more step to overcome in your pursuit of a life of fulfillment. It's all a process of learning more about who you are. You might feel frustrated at times, but stay curious as you uncover and learn more. Allow each beaten fear to fuel and strengthen your inner voice. Pass the baton from fear to courage, allowing yourself not to choose out of fear but to choose *for your-*

self. Fear only has power when you give yours away. Give yourself time, space, and permission to unravel all the stories you have written. Regain your strength a little bit with each new narrative. This will bring you closer to the acceptance you need to choose the life you want.

If you're not feeling even a teensy bit scared of the choice you want to make, you're not dreaming big enough (or perhaps you picked up the wrong book). Transformational life choices are scary AF. Letting go of the life you know and stepping into the life you want is hard…*at first*. It's hard because we've been conditioned to fit society's mould, but when you choose to build your own, it comes without an instruction manual. You get to figure things out as you go, and while it might feel hard in the middle of it, it's all worth it on the other side, I can assure you.

The first choice to change is the most challenging, but each choice that follows becomes easier as you start living a life of fulfillment. So if you're not feeling the tummy flips or insecurities or questioning if you can do this thing, you're playing small—go bigger! (Or maybe you're Superwoman, which would be *super* cool!) These steps don't apply to small shifts or day-to-day changes. This framework applies to the transformational choices that have the potential to change your world.

The Full Embrace

A cceptance. What does it feel like? When we accept our desire to choose a more fulfilling life, it feels good in our bodies and puts us at ease. I do not associate acceptance with defeat, which is deciding to see your circumstances as unchangeable. Nope, that, my friends, is an excuse to avoid making the choice you need to reach greater fulfillment.

The kind of acceptance I'm referring to is felt with a full heart. It's like giving yourself a warm hug. You feel safe and content, and everything feels right in the world. Acceptance brings you closer and closer to the belief that you *can* choose change and that you are on the right path.

This is what acceptance felt like for me: It was fleeting, but it was there and proved to me that I was moving in the right direction. Battling fear after fear was tough, but necessary. I had to accept that fear would never disappear completely. I learned the goal was not to seek out a fearless state where you have all the courage and none of the resistance. That state doesn't exist; fear will always be present. It's scary to choose yourself because it's likely not something you do enough. I know it wasn't easy for me.

My bravery grew out of rewriting those fear stories. It took focused energy to dissect what those stories meant, and I had to know myself enough to understand what was holding me back. When we can see our fears as stories, it brings us closer to acceptance. The beautiful thing about stories is that they can be rewritten. I rewrote many of my fear stories, which allowed me to gain confidence and believe that I could step away from the life that was draining me. Resistance still lingered, but I was feeling more ready to act and fully embrace that nudge on my heart.

I had to do two things in the acceptance stage, and both helped me embrace my decision to leave my job. First, I had to write my resignation letter. This letter would give me another nudge toward certainty. Second, I had to quiet the gremlins in my mind, the incessant thoughts that kept saying, *I don't know what to do*. I knew what I had to do; I was just resisting because I was scared.

My resignation letter was something that needed to be written if I did decide to quit. When I sat down to write it, I needed to take some pressure off, so I told myself I didn't have to use it if I changed my mind. No one would know I had written it. This provided me the space I needed to write it without attachment, to see how it felt.

I couldn't remember what information went into a resignation letter at the time, but Google is a great invention, and within thirty minutes I had found a template and completed the letter. What I felt in that moment was a sense of calm. I didn't feel scared, sad, anxious, or nervous about what the letter represented, and writing it felt easy. That ease comforted me, and it felt like a sign. This choice was beginning to feel like it was the right one in a bigger and bigger way.

When I felt that sense of calm after writing my resignation letter, I felt empowered that I could do this. Every stage prior had been super challenging, and I was getting tired. That feeling of calm gave me a renewed strength. I didn't have to stay where I was and suffer just for the sake of a job title. I could choose differently and desire something else, even if it wasn't going to make sense to everyone else.

We are conditioned by our families, by greater society, and by the media that life is supposed to be hard and that, if it's not hard, we're not doing it right. I disagree. When life is hard, it means we are out of alignment. It means we are forcing ourselves to show up in the wrong ways and in the wrong places. Life is supposed to be fulfilling! So let's check that belief at the door, along with your doubts and fears, and choose fulfillment. Cool? Okay, cool. Let's keep going.

We are meant to enjoy life with ease and with grace. Whenever I've followed what feels good in my heart (not what provides the least resistance), I've had some of my best experiences or have had breakthroughs that changed my life. And most often, those decisions were made with emotion and not with logic.

When we are in tune with our bodies, we can feel how a particular decision, person, or opportunity resonates. When we're not in tune with our bodies, this isn't as easy. But there are a number of simple indicators that you can take note of to see how something feels. A tightness in your chest or shortness of breath likely means you're straying from your highest self. Anxiety and stress are huge indicators—we've been trained to think these are normal, but this is not our natural state. You may also get knots in your shoulders, neck, or lower back. Signs like these show you that your body is telling you something—maybe you should listen for a change. One of my fail-safe triggers is my right shoulder blade. When that little guy flares up, I know I need to do some reflecting.

If you're not into the body feels, that's cool because you also have emotions, and your emotions are also strong messengers. Emotions also help you move through tough decisions. You simply need to acknowledge when the good vibrations come through during times of struggle. I already described numerous struggles that I experienced during this process, so when I reached acceptance, this was a huge milestone; I had reached a place of ease. It was key that I recognized that. The fact that I didn't feel afraid when writing my resignation letter spoke volumes. Don't get me wrong, handing in my resignation gave me the tummy flips, but writing it felt right. By focusing on that feeling and not getting too far ahead, I was able to welcome the feeling of acceptance coming my way. This continued to give me courage and help me take one more step toward following my heart and choosing myself.

Trusting those feelings is key. Those glimpses of contentment, acceptance, and ease mean you are on the right track and give you the best indication there is that you are following your true path, a path that supports what your heart truly desires.

I want to take an extra moment to really emphasize what the feeling of acceptance feels like, because as I said, our fears never disappear—they will only dissipate. It's important that you notice when you reach your full embrace. It's a beautiful and profound moment when you finally feel good about choosing yourself. The moment when you finally believe you are worthy. It's an experience I never want you to forget. It might even be the first time you've felt like enough in a long time.

I want you to acknowledge and celebrate this because you are worthy of it, and you have finally recognized your true worth. Your dreams and your life matter. Your dreams are an undeniable truth that is meant for you. When you choose yourself, you will be amazed at how many others start to see your worth too. Embrace these feelings, this renewed acceptance and love for yourself. You might need to revisit this moment before you finally take that big leap.

I didn't embody my feelings of acceptance when they first came to me because they were fleeting. I might have even missed this stage completely if I didn't have my journal by my side. This is why I want to emphasize how important it is to acknowledge your full embrace. This is when you will start to feel ready to act.

With my brief state of calm and ease, I caught my breath. I reverted to logic and tried to justify why I could and should quit my job. It still didn't make sense though. At the end of the day, these types of decisions might not be logical, and they aren't always going to make sense on paper, so we can't force them to make sense. But they *will* feel right in your heart and you will know you made the right choice. Your future self will thank you as they look back from your more fulfilling life.

When I look back at some of the bigger decisions I've made in life—travelling solo across Southeast Asia for months, ending a relationship with the person I thought I would marry, and then quitting my professional job—I realize these decisions weren't made logically. They were soul decisions, decisions I knew I had to make, no matter how intense, heartbreaking, or uncertain the outcome might be. They ended up being the best decisions I ever made. They gave me the opportunity for the most growth, and they helped me step into exactly who I am meant to be. It's time for you to step into who you are meant to be too.

Despite my sense of calm, I still had lingering naysaying thoughts in my brain. I was feeling more certain, but I was still scared, scared that I would make the wrong decision.

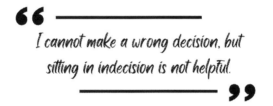

I cannot make a wrong decision, but sitting in indecision is not helpful.

My life coach reminded me around this time that, no matter what choice I made, I could not eff this up, but it was important that I did decide. I needed this shift in perspective to help cut through the remaining threads of uncertainty I still had. I knew what was best for me, and it was time to listen to myself. I would either thrive, learn, or, at the very least, I would be moving forward.

There are lessons in each and every experience you have. Some experiences will bring you closer to the life you want, and others will show you what you don't want. It's not a failure if something doesn't turn out the way you expect; it's a lesson for you to learn from. I encourage you to remain open to learning and trust that no matter what decision you make, it's the right one at the time. We are all doing the best we can with the information we have, but sitting in indecision gets us nowhere. So make a choice and own it wholeheartedly. No more sitting half in/half out anymore.

When I accepted that I could not eff this up, it reduced the mountain of pressure I was putting on myself to make the *right* choice. If I couldn't make the wrong decision, all I had to do was make *a* decision. Right? And so it pushed me to make a choice. I had agonized long enough, and I needed to shit or get off the pot. I mean, I wrote the resignation letter, didn't I? It felt good, didn't it? I had tackled my fears, right? Was I really going to turn back now?

It sounds simple when I write it like that, but deep down I was really struggling with feelings of indecision, and the phrase "I don't know what to do" was stuck on repeat in my head. I learned that sitting in indecision was a special kind of torture, and it's definitely not going to serve you. You'll likely sit in it longer than necessary with the same fear I had, scared to make the wrong choice. It's okay to still be afraid, but the quicker we can decide and accept what we already know in our hearts, the sooner we will reach greater fulfillment. The answers are inside you and you will always know what is best; it's up to you to cut through the noise around you, let your inner voice be heard, and allow indecision to fade away.

With my resignation letter written and a newfound confidence that I couldn't make a wrong decision, I was feeling more prepared to leave my job. I knew I would have been letting myself down if I chose to stay because this role wasn't the right fit for me anymore. I would have been disappointed in myself if I didn't use the courage I knew I had to follow through.

I want to share a deeper truth right now: I knew from the very beginning. I knew that I needed to quit. What I didn't know was if I had the strength to make the choice. I had to go through each step to embrace it in full. From the moment I first thought about quitting, it was inevitable for me. And I believe whatever choice you are considering or struggling to make, that it is inevitable for you too. You deserve happiness and to live the life you desire; all you need is the confidence (that already lives inside you!) to believe you can do it. I don't believe life is meant to be hard, and neither should you. Remember, we checked that belief at the door earlier.

Throughout our lives, we encounter a tonne of bigger life choices, and they all start out as thoughts. Some we sweep aside or tuck away, and others we act on. It's the thoughts and choices that keep returning that you need to listen to; they will lead you to your higher purpose and greater fulfillment. This one kept coming back for me until I was ready to act on it. I knew deep in my heart from the moment my catalyst struck that staying at that job would leave me unhappy and unfulfilled. I had to walk through these struggles to accept that I was allowed to choose something different, and believe it on all levels.

You also have a deeper truth, a knowing, I'm sure of it. Something is nestled deep in your heart that you desire. You might be ignoring it or refusing to listen. I get it—I ignored my whispers too. That's how we are conditioned. It's our natural response when a possibility or dream isn't paired with certainty, but instead tethered to the unknown. But you already know what you want. You have already thought about it! I can guarantee it. You've just been too afraid to consider that it could become real, too afraid to believe it's possible. I'm here to tell you it is possible—if you choose it.

We all know when a job, a relationship, or a situation doesn't truly serve us, but we continually try to convince ourselves otherwise. We feel it in our bodies and dwell on it constantly, sometimes so much that it makes us sick. If we could learn to listen to ourselves sooner and embrace the fact that we can't make a wrong decision, we could lead more fulfilling lives with ease. But this requires intention and active decision-making. That is the only way to thrive or learn the lessons we are meant to. Decide, choose, and follow through.

I believe that we need to feel ready to make these transformational moves, and I know that that will look different for each of us. You may feel ready for a minute and then retreat into the stages of fear or doubt. This is normal, and I do not want you to look at it as a regression if it happens to you. If you take a step back, it's likely because you haven't addressed something from those stages yet. We can't rush our healing or our knowing. Your choice must be made when you are ready to own it. It's up to you to wholeheartedly choose what you want. If you're not there yet, keep digging into why—just don't dig yourself all the way to China. Remember, you are worthy of a life you want, and it's time to choose it. Don't wait and keep your life on pause, living in mediocrity. You can reach for more.

And keep in mind that the beauty and struggle of every decision is that you can change your mind. You can choose to move in one direction, see how things play out, and, if it doesn't fit, you can make a new choice. Life is full of choices, but you have to make them! And don't kid yourself by staying in a life that doesn't serve you or that leaves you unhappy at the end of the day. That is also a choice. Don't think for a second that you don't have some semblance of control over your life. Don't blame others for your hardships or circumstances. When you stay in the hard space, you are *choosing* to stay there. It will be no one's fault but your own if you wake up five or ten years down the road in exactly the same spot you are in today. It's your life, your choice. Are you ready to choose fulfillment yet?

That deep inner knowing is your truth. Give it room

to grow and be heard, and soon you will feel ready. Well, as ready as you will ever be, because it's always going to feel scary! It's time to move forward and trade the hard you know for the hard you choose. I'm not going to tell you that after you choose to change your life the next steps are going to be easy. There will be more learnings and different hardships, but there will also be moments of complete ecstasy and elation, feelings you didn't realize you could feel. I guarantee everything will feel better because you'll be experiencing it with *you* at the centre.

Embrace the feelings of acceptance, because you won't be out of the woods just yet. You care about others, just like I do, and will worry about how they will be impacted by your choice. This is when guilt creeps in and forms a final hurdle to overcome.

Guilt

As social beings, our social ties are incredibly important. We nurture and grow these connections in a variety of ways, and we care for others. This level of care, though, can become a barrier to our own happiness because, instead of prioritizing what brings us a sense of fulfillment, we put others' needs first and prioritize their happiness. When we act in this way, we are saying that others matter more than we do. Each time you do something for someone else that hinders your fulfillment, you are saying that that person matters more than you. When we put others first the majority of the time, we will actually feel guilty when we do something for ourselves. We worry about how our decisions will affect others around us. But what about the effect they have on *us*? What about putting on our own oxygen masks first? What if we started to give ourselves that first leg up before supporting everyone else around us? Would we not be stronger, wiser, happier, and more fulfilled? Would that not allow us to show up for others as the best versions of ourselves and share all the bright light and energy we possess?

I believe in putting myself first, but I still felt guilty for leaving my job. I didn't want to let people down, and so I had to break down my own guilty feelings.

Once I decided to leave my job and embraced that decision, the reality of my choice began to unravel in my heart and mind. At this stage, I was no longer worried about the effect the choice would have on me and my life—I was excited for what was in store. Now I was concerned about how my decision would impact other people directly. We are connected beings, and our decisions have a ripple effect on those around us. There is no way to comprehend the full impact of our decisions, but when we live into our best selves, we have more to give to those around us. Start your ripple with a full heart and with a choice of fulfillment. For me, I know that a fulfilled Sara is the most inspiring and authentic version of myself, and that is the version I wanted to be.

Even with this belief in my heart and acceptance in my mind, I still carried a heavy weight, knowing I would disappoint people. I felt guilty for leaving my team and even more so for leaving a boss and mentor who had nurtured me into a strong leader. Without my boss, it would have taken me much longer to believe in my capabilities.

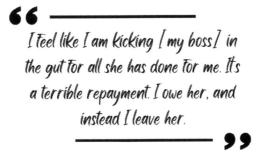

I feel like I am kicking [my boss] in the gut for all she has done for me. It's a terrible repayment. I owe her, and instead I leave her.

This journal entry expresses the guilt I was feeling. I felt like I was being ungrateful by making this choice and like I was letting down a person for whom I had a great amount of respect. Finally, I carried the weight that I owed my boss for the things she had done for me. I had to unpack these feelings.

"I'M BEING UNGRATEFUL."

Why did I feel ungrateful? I felt ungrateful because of the growth opportunities I had been given. I felt as if, by leaving, I was dismissing the support I had received from the organization and my boss. With their support, I had started to believe in my potential. Now I just wanted to start using it in my own way. Was that so wrong? I now believed in my own abilities and wanted to use those gifts wholeheartedly. My boss saw my potential way before I did, and I am beyond grateful for her vision. I had to understand that I wasn't being ungrateful by choosing to leave; I was finally embracing what she saw in me all along. By choosing myself, I wasn't leaving her in the dust with a peace sign in the air. I was saying "thank you" for helping me see what I was capable of all along, telling her that now I saw it too and I wanted to forge my own path. I was able to flip feeling ungrateful into feeling thankful for all that was given to me.

"I'M LETTING OTHERS DOWN."

Every strong organization has a succession plan, and for this foundation, I was it. They wanted to help me grow so I could become the next CEO. But at one point I had to ask, *Do I want to be the next CEO?* There was a time when I had felt excited—and admittedly a little terrified—that I could be offered this leadership role. I had even been told that the Board of Governors believed I was capable. What an honour. As time passed and I began to listen to the calling on my heart though, I realized that becoming the next CEO, whether that occurred in six months or five years, wasn't what I truly wanted, capable or not. I didn't want that job anymore.

This awareness truly dawned on me when my boss told me she had been approached to consider two new positions. She had turned down both positions, but it made me think, *What if she had accepted?* She would have left her role as head of the foundation and I would have stepped in as interim—maybe permanent—CEO. I had to get out before I couldn't. I knew that if I was given that role at any time, I wouldn't be strong enough to walk away from it. I would have carried the weight of that organization on my shoulders and carried it proudly. But I knew it wasn't the role that was going to leave me fulfilled, and I wouldn't do the role justice if my heart wasn't in it. I needed to leave before that could happen.

By choosing to leave, I felt like I was letting not only the Board and my boss down, but also the team I worked with each day and every community I was supporting. I felt a personal responsibility to each of them and I felt that, by leaving, I was abandoning them.

What helped was changing my point of view—I put myself in their shoes. If any one of these people had come to me and asked me if they should follow their heart or expressed that they were no longer feeling fulfilled in their role, I wouldn't have hesitated to support them. I would have said with a resounding and absolute "yes" that they needed to follow their dreams. I luckily received nothing but support from the team and organization after announcing my departure. Many were disappointed that I was leaving, but not one person made me feel guilty or made me feel like I was letting them down. They genuinely wanted me to do what was best for me, and they respected my decision.

You aren't letting people down when you choose yourself, because if others truly care for you, they want you to be happy. It's up to you to choose your happiness and fulfillment or any other desire you have in your heart, because no one else will choose it for you. You must live your life for yourself, without the worry of letting others down, and instead worry about letting *yourself* down.

"I OWE THEM."

This was a heavy one, and I would bet big money that you've felt this feeling before. I'm going to be straight with you, though. It does not matter what anyone else has done for you; you don't owe them anything. You just don't. And here's why.

At no point along the way did you force or coerce people into helping or supporting you. Did I force my boss to support my professional development? Did I force her to give me promotions? Did I force the Board to see my potential? No to all of the above. I am so grateful that they did those things for me, but in no way did I force that support from them. They made those choices and invested in me because they believed in me. I am endlessly thankful for that. My relationships with these people weren't meant to be transactional; they were relational. We forged connections over time. When we support and connect with one another as people, and not as investments or power moves, we elevate one another together.

Now I want you to think about a situation where

you felt like you owed someone else. At any point did you *force* them to help you out? Whether we're talking about your parents, a partner, friends, mentors, bosses, or anyone, was there any point where you forced them to do something for you or support you in some way? My best guess is no. You might have asked for support, money, care, or understanding, but you didn't force anyone to give those things to you. Others have the power to make the decisions that they do. The same goes for all the wonderful things we do for others; we do them because we choose to, not because we have to.

There's an important point to be made here. There is a difference between feeling like we owe someone and allowing it to hold us back versus acknowledging and appreciating what people have done for us. We can feel grateful for all the ways others have supported us and still choose a different path. We do not owe others for the kindness they have offered.

Others might have opinions or their own reasons for wanting you to stay where you are, and they are entitled to their thoughts, but that doesn't mean you have to accept their opinions that you should stay. You have the right to put yourself first, and you don't have to forfeit your happiness out of guilt.

If people choose not to respect you for stepping into your truth, or if they hold their kindness over your head like you weren't worthy of it from the start, politely wave goodbye with your middle finger up. You don't have time for that kind of non-supportive nonsense. You are worthy—you just finally realized it yourself. Don't step back, step *up!* The support of others may have helped you get to where you are; appreciate and acknowledge that, but also realize that you had it inside of you all along. It's time to own that.

Not allowing guilt to weigh you down will be one of the last challenges you will work to overcome. The truth is that there is no way to truly avoid letting someone down. It is not a matter of *if* you let someone down, but *who,* and who you let down is up to you. The choice is between you or other people. You can choose to be weighed down by the guilt of letting others down, or you can carry the weight of letting yourself down. Either way, you will carry some guilt, and I ask you, do you want to continue to allow others to dictate your life or do you want to take control of it? What would you tell someone else making this choice?

Guilt is heavy, but the guilt of not choosing yourself will weigh heavier. It's not fair when others' needs are always proclaimed to be more important than your own. You are worthy. So I wonder, *what would it take for you to choose yourself?*

The guilt you feel in relation to others will subside because you know deep down that you are not abandoning them; you are simply choosing yourself. You deserve to be chosen as much as anyone else. You are equally as important! So stop putting others first all the damn time. Choosing yourself will always be the right choice. I had to remind myself of that before I called my boss and made it all real.

THE CALL TO MY BOSS

After all my processing, the conversations, the tears, and the agonizing feels, it was time to step up and make my decision real. I had to tell my boss I was leaving. I didn't have the space or the strength to live in both realities anymore. I couldn't turn back either. I was no longer committed to my job and was now committed to me. Not choosing myself was no longer an option. I had a duty to finally step up and choose myself.

After agonizing over this decision, I gathered my courage and took action.

With no concrete plan, no other job in sight, in the midst of a global pandemic, I quit my stable, high-paying, management-level, professionally supportive job. Am I crazy? Maybe to some, but when we feel pulled in a new direction, for something greater, we have to make those calls that make no sense to anyone else.

I had a lead anchor in my gut the morning I called

my boss. I had to tell a woman I respected more than anything that I was leaving, effectively turning down the opportunity for continued growth and an inevitably successful career. I was shaking, and it took all I had to keep my voice from quivering as I said, "I've decided to leave."

Silence

I had this punch-in-the-gut feeling the moment those words left my lips. I had just made it real. My boss was in complete shock and disbelief and asked, "Are you sure? Do you have another job?" That's what made this even more unexplainable to her and so many others. I didn't have another job or a clear path ahead, but I was sure. I wouldn't have made that call without that certainty.

It will take certainty and courage to make that bold step, even more so when you don't have the next step figured out. While that phone rang, every fear story reeled through me once again. This was why it was so key for me to take the time to go through each previous step before making that call. Overwhelm. Doubt. Taking space. Fear. Acceptance. Guilt. They all had their roles to play that brought me closer to choosing myself and, most importantly, gave me the courage to stick to it.

The remainder of the conversation with my boss was a blur, but I remember I could barely keep it together. I was unbelievably thankful I was able to have the conversation over the phone—we were in the middle of the pandemic and in-person interaction wasn't really a thing at the time. I had to dig deep not to burst into tears that day. I knew leaving was the right call, but that didn't make the choice any easier, nor was the message any easier to deliver. I had to remind myself of the emotional turmoil I had just walked through to get to this decision. Each stage represented a new challenge and a new wound that I had to treat and heal. I was fragile, but also the strongest I've ever been.

It's a duality you might live through too when you decide to take your leap—feeling fragile yet strong at the same time. The beauty in this leap is you are going to be able to count on yourself. You won't have to worry if you will fall because you can trust that you will be there to catch yourself.

Let Yourself Fly

When you think about jumping off the metaphorical cliff into new possibilities, you're naturally going to think about the inevitable fall. Can you picture your arms flailing and grasping at the air around you but not slowing you down? The butterflies that hit your tummy and the struggle to fill your lungs with air? For anyone who has gone bungee jumping or cliff diving or simply jumped off a set of swings, you'll know the feeling I'm talking about.

But what if, instead of falling, you could fly?

What if, instead of thinking you have no control over what's next, you felt the wind catch you and you soared? You soared high and glided across the sky toward freedom and openness. You had complete control over where you would land and could see for miles along the horizon. Isn't that a more exhilarating story to tell yourself? Instead of falling to the pits, you would get to soar like a freaking eagle! When choosing fulfillment, you're still going to get those butterflies and fear the initial jump, but once your feet leave that edge, you'll be free and ready to fly. Don't you want to fly?

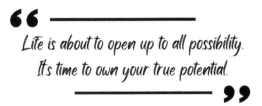

> *Life is about to open up to all possibility.*
> *It's time to own your true potential.*

I knew that by leaving my job I was giving myself the opportunity to fly, and it was definitely the most feel-good part of the process. Taking the leap put me in my highest vibration. I chose myself. I proved to myself that I was worthy enough to be chosen. I dismissed other people's fears, I tackled my own doubts, and I left behind that thing that was dimming my light. My light and my energy are a huge part of who I am, the essence that people crave and want to be around. Without those, I was simply existing. When I chose to release my ties, I was bringing myself back to who I fundamentally was and who I wanted to be. I felt lighter. The heaviness of the stress and overwhelm melted away, and I felt excited about next steps, whatever those turned out to be.

When we let things go, we make space in our life for new things to come in. Let yourself fly, and shed the weight that is holding you back.

Do you need to let go of that relationship? The one you've poured your heart and soul into but that now feels empty—release and let go, and trust you did everything you could without losing yourself. Are you tired of grinding so hard for someone else and ready to start your own thing? At some point you need to get rid of the safety net. Have you put off that surgery you need because the recovery time is too lengthy for your liking? Focus on the rewards after you're healed and release the attachment to the short-term. Whatever is holding you back, stop allowing it to keep you stuck in a life you don't truly love. It's necessary to release the ties to the old life that is no longer serving you. Mentally, physically, emotionally and spiritually, release the anchors weighing you down in this old stale life. When you choose fulfillment, you will stop simply existing and you will start living. One of my favourite sayings of all time is you only live once, or "YOLO." Keep that in mind and lean into the feeling of possibility.

I gave six weeks' notice to wrap up my job instead of the typical two because my role was quite complex. I cared too much about the organization, the team, and my boss to up and leave on a dime. I also had the freedom and flexibility to choose that. If you need a clean break and to GTFO stat, do what's best for you. A longer transition might not be best for you or for everyone involved. Remember, this is your journey and your life. Choose accordingly.

To wrap up my role, I had one rather large task I wanted to complete. In all the years I had worked in this role, we *(*cough* I)* had never documented the policies or procedures of our programs. Who wanted to spend time creating training manuals when you could be out building a playground? These were the actual choices I had. Given the length of time I ran each program and the freedom I was given to make them my own, I implemented many of my own practices and ways of doing things that worked best for me. The challenge was that I was the only one who knew how to do run these programs…for the most part. This was the benefit and downfall of working in a small organization.

Knowing there was a major knowledge gap in the team when it came to my role, I was determined to close this gap before leaving. I wanted to create a training binder for my replacement. I wanted it to include the background of each program, day-to-day ins and outs, tracking and spreadsheets, and the important milestones to keep track of throughout the year. *This was a task and a half!* It took me almost a full month of working full time to put this together. I felt incredibly proud of myself for completing it, and handing that binder over made me feel like I had wrapped up my job with a bright red bow.

In addition to running the entire program side of the foundation, I had also been leading numerous park projects and needed to transfer those to another team member. Each time I transferred something else over, I let go of a little more responsibility. My ties were being cut, one conversation at a time. And each time it got a little stressful and I was reminded how much work there was to do, I'd think of one of my favourite sayings, "Not my circus, not my monkeys." I'd take a deep breath, smile, and let it go. These projects were no longer something I had to worry about and *Oooooh*, what a satisfying feeling that was! And each time this happened, it reminded me that I had made the right choice. I was feeling lighter and lighter each day, allowing me to really lean into fulfillment as I finished up my role.

It's super important as you transition and cut ties from your old life that you focus forward and feel the excited feels about your decision. Don't focus on what you're leaving behind because you've already decided to move forward. So, if you're choosing to go back to work after having kids, get excited about leaving the house again. If you're newly single and the simple thought of dating scares you, date yourself instead! Take yourself on all the awesome dates you've always wanted. Want to write that book, start that blog, or create that YouTube channel? Just *start!* Get playful and do it for fun. And if you're not sure what to get excited about, simply celebrate your dang self for making it through this process and choosing yourself. All you have to do moving forward is continue choosing your-self each and every day.

In order to fly free, you need to let go. Release what held you back and then welcome in all the possibilities about your next chapter. What is it that you need to let go of? We have crafted these ties and weighted these anchors in place over a significant period, so be kind to yourself as you work to release and let go. Remember, let go first, then fly.

During my final weeks, I was asked on numerous occasions how I was feeling about my decision. People asked, *"Are you sure?"* Some even asked, *"Do you think they would take you back if you changed your mind?"* *Psssh,* I didn't know because I didn't want to stay—and you want to know the *best* part? There was not one single moment after I took the leap where I questioned my decision. I did not feel one iota of regret because I chose *me*. I was free.

That is what's so beautiful and necessary about going through each one of these steps. The dreaded lows and crappy feels don't last. Trust me. I feared many times that I would get stuck in those hard moments and didn't want to let it all in. But it wasn't until I let the hard feelings in that I could move past them. I promise, you won't get stuck, so feel everything you need to feel.

From my initial catalyst to the moment I gave my notice, less than a month had passed, and the majority of my deep reflection happened over the course of two weeks. I'll admit, each day during those two weeks felt like a month. The struggle was real, but the journey through it brought me to a spot where I could make my decision with certainty. I spent the time necessary in the lows so I could make my choice without hesitation. By navigating your emotions, doubts, and fears on your path to choosing fulfillment, you uncover and create a deeper connection to yourself. You've chosen to ask what you want, and you've chosen to listen. Deep down, you know it's right; you've always known it was right, and in the end, you won't question your decision —you will celebrate it.

Now I want to remind you that I didn't know what I was going to do when I left my job. I didn't have a plan. So try not to get caught in the trap of thinking you need to have it all figured out. This isn't AA. Choosing to change your life doesn't happen with a twelve-step program. Rather, you're writing your own program, with each step and each decision to choose you. It might feel a little scarier if you don't have a plan right away, but sometimes life requires us to take the leap first. We have to let go of the things that are holding us back to create room for the good to come in. By loosening our white-knuckled grip on our current circumstance, we not only allow the universe to show up for us, we also trust that it will. The steps that come after will appear, I promise.

You weren't born to stay small; you were born to rise up. You weren't born to shy away; you were born to step up. You weren't born to live an average life; you were born for an extraordinary one. It's time to get unstuck and surrender to the life you were born to live. It's okay to let go of what was. Our lives aren't meant to stay the same. We are meant to learn lessons, take risks, and live life! *We're* not meant to stay the same forever, and neither are the people who surround us. Others are meant to change too. We might long for what was or how things used to be, but newsflash, things will never be like they used to be. Nothing will ever be the same. Each day we are changing. We can't stop this process, so why not embrace it instead? Stop looking back and start looking forward. Break free of the cage you have put yourself in and let yourself fly.

Conclusion

I f you're not sure where to start on this journey or you feel like there are numerous places you want to bring deeper meaning to your life, I invite you to sit down and close your eyes. Take five deep belly breaths and ask yourself, "Where do I desire fulfillment most right now?" The first answer will be the right answer. Start there.

Choosing fulfillment is a choice. It doesn't come to us when we passively wait for it to show up on our doorstep. When our lives don't reflect what we want, it is our responsibility to choose change; otherwise, we are simply choosing to stay stuck. Not choosing what you want is as much a choice as stepping into something new. And something new requires bold and transformational moves.

Don't be fooled and think that stepping away from the life you know is going to be easy. It's agonizing . . . at first. It's super emotional to step away from what you know. Even if the life you have is hard, it's a hard you know. It can feel easier to stay where you know what to expect, even if it's not what you want. It's harder to make a bold choice to choose something different, *especially* if you don't have the next steps figured out. But don't you want to reclaim your life and start living it for you, on your terms?

This choice was one of the most challenging decisions I've ever made in my life—because it wasn't logical. If I had had another job lined up, no problem, I'd just be shifting gears. If I had decided to start a consulting business, I'd be an entrepreneur! That would have been pretty exciting. If I had planned to take time off and travel for six months, that would have been an adventure, and everyone around me would have understood my choice just a little bit more—because I "had a plan." But I had none of that. I didn't know what my next steps were; I just had a whisper and an inkling that I wanted to spend some time writing. I gave myself permission not to worry about next steps. And I grant you the same.

One thing I did know for certain was that I didn't have space in my life, in my heart, or in my mind to allow anything else in while I stayed at that job. I was tapped out on all fronts, and even the thought of coming up with a plan made me feel overwhelmed. I needed to step away from the things that were draining me first to create space and explore what made me happy. I took a chance and trusted that things would come together. Deep down I knew they would, but it took a lot of faith in the universe to trust that every-thing was going to be okay.

It all started with a spark, my catalyst—two uncon-trollable sobbing fits that made me realize something had to change. I had to stop pretending that I was okay and acknowledge that I was overworked and no longer fulfilled. I always wanted—and still want—an extraordinary life. Coasting through life without adven-ture, exploration, and growth wasn't acceptable to me, and never will be again.

Is it acceptable to you? You are only on this planet, in this body, and in this life once. Don't you want to live the best life you can? Isn't the purpose of life to live it?

I wasn't living the life I wanted, but I doubted that I could have something different. I doubted that I was worthy of something better because, according to soci-ety, what I had was pretty damn good. Was I really going to give that up? The truth is that it doesn't matter what things look like on paper or what other people think. What matters is how we feel inside. We are the ones who have to live our lives, day in and day out.

I doubted that I could go off on my own into the unknown, and my fears were powerful. This entire experience required me to take a hard look at the stories I was telling myself. Other people were scared for me, too—it was confusing and hard for them to understand why I would take such a leap, especially during a global pandemic!

I gave myself the gift of space. This act reset me and brought me a renewed sense of clarity. It might feel hard to find that separation, or to create distance, but you need to find it. Getting away from the life we're used to gives us the opportunity to think without outside pressure.

Acceptance gave me a quick reprieve from my emotional agony, and it fuelled my strength. It supported me and told me my choice was the right one. The final stage of resistance comes from our loving spirit, which makes us worry about how our choices could affect other people. I didn't want to let anyone down, but I also couldn't accept disappointing myself. Your needs, wants, and desires matter as much as everyone else's, so remember that you matter too. I did. I quit my perfect-on-paper job without a plan, and I chose to open myself up to new possibilities. When you let go, you set yourself free and you put yourself on the trajectory toward fulfillment.

There are endless scenarios that might guide you to consider something different for your life, and these pages reflect what I experienced on my journey. I had to let go of what others expected or wanted me to do and find trust. The journey to your dreams might look different, and the time you spend in each stage is also going to be completely unique to you. It's likely you won't even notice when you move from stage to stage;

they might blur together, or one stage might feel never-ending. There is no one-size-fits-all to choosing fulfillment.

A different catalyst might propel you into this cycle of self-discovery. You will also battle with self-doubt and fight fear. Guilt might weigh you down, but as you move through each one of these steps, you will find yourself on your path to purpose—a path that will lead you toward a life you really want—so don't give up.

What I can say for certain is this: Choosing yourself is scary. Choosing a life that others don't understand is hard. Navigating a path without a compass is rough. Despite everything I walked through though, I don't have one single regret.

This is what you can expect when you choose your dreams and start on your own path toward a life of fulfillment. It's not going to feel easy to choose yourself at first, and it's not supposed to. It will be hard and it will be challenging to step into the unknown, without a parachute, without your safety net, and without the understanding of those around you. This is why it is vital to build trust in yourself and remind yourself that, when you waver, you've got this. You might dip back into some of the feelings described in the previous chapters, but you'll be able to move through them with more ease and come out stronger each time because you know you matter too.

Our deeper desires are a reflection into our souls, which is why your vision might not make sense to others around you. And it doesn't have to. What fills you up is unlikely to fill up the next person. We are all different, and that's why it's important for you to craft your own way forward. You can no longer put other peoples' comfort and opinions first if you want to achieve a fulfilled life. And that is hard AF, but it's a hard you get to choose.

I lost connection to myself and my work at a deeper level. That's what started this whole thing. I declined fast as I became more aware that I was out of alignment. I had to let go of my safety net and stop believing that my circumstances were unchangeable. Instead, I had to choose courage and choose differently.

I didn't know where I was going to end up, and I'll be honest, the endless unknowns almost prevented me from quitting my job. I had to guide myself into the unknown even though it felt scary. My job provided me security and certainty, and my ego wanted me to hold on to it tightly. It took extraordinary intention to actively step away from what was deemed safe and from what others considered acceptable. I no longer held on to the traditional view of success and instead moved toward a life fulfilled.

For many years, I loved my job and it was incredibly fulfilling. I felt fortunate to be one of the few who got to get up in the morning and look forward to what they did. But why the heck is that the anomaly? Why is desiring and choosing a fulfilled state not encouraged? Why do we accept that a life of stress and anxiety is the norm? We're taught that we should be grateful for what we have—and we should be—but that doesn't mean we have to roll over and accept that this is all there is. You are allowed to want more.

We can hold space for our current lives *and* want more *and* choose differently. We can't continue thinking that our lives are an either/or scenario. We can do what we love *and* be financially stable. We can embrace our relationship status *and* desire more. We can have kids *and* have our dream jobs. We can have freedom *and* have a perfect home. We can support ourselves *and* live out our dreams. *And, and, and.*

There might be things in your life right now that you still love or have a strong attachment to, things you are scared to let go of. This will be one of the biggest things holding you back. Instead of focusing on what you might (though it's never 100% guaranteed) leave behind, envision what you *can* have. What feels good? Where are you being pulled? Do you want to hold on to those things you still love that light you up only once a year, or do you want to shine all year round?

A life fulfilled is a choice, but it's also your right. You don't have to let go of everything. I still have a great relationship with my boss because I think she is one of the best humans out there. Leaving her was one of the hardest parts of making my decision, but it wasn't enough to make me stay. So remember, you don't have to leave every piece behind—you might just need to change how you stay connected to it. It's also possible that you step away completely. It's okay to move on and let go.

We are meant to feel happy and abundant and live with ease, not in a constant state of fear, stress, and overwhelm. You can choose to hold on to the life you have and the version of who you are now, or you can dig in and choose boldly. It's in your power to have a fulfilled life, but you have to choose it. You might not feel like you have the strength to take a big leap, but if this book is in your hands, I believe you have what it takes. Your purpose for being on this earth is linked solely to you. It's a purpose that no one else can fulfill, and the world needs you to own that purpose.

By choosing a life of fulfillment, you empower others to do the same. And if you remember anything, remember this: there is only one you, and there are things in this world that only you can do. I believe in you, even if you don't just yet. I can't wait for you to change the life you have into the life you want.

About the Author

As a personal development nerd, Sara is always diving into her depths and strives to fall in love with who she is becoming. Through her social media presence, personal blog, and 1:1 coaching, she guides others to courageously seek lives they desire.

Sara calls Calgary, Alberta her home, which she also honours and recognizes as Mohkinstsis (MOH-kin-stiss), the Blackfoot name for Calgary, meaning "elbow" in reference to the Elbow River. As a white settler living on the traditional lands of Treaty 7 territory, and in the spirit of truth and reconciliation, she acknowledges those who inhabited this land before her.

As an experience enthusiast, Sara has a true love for travel, and she might also impress you with her tolerance for red wine. You can find Sara on Instagram

@TheOnlySaraStepa for inspiration on the daily. She is also the author and creator of a blog called The Attitude Is Gratitude, where she encourages her followers to dream without barriers. To sign up for her blog or to be coached by Sara, visit www.theattitudeisgratitude.ca.

Thank You For Reading!

With the fullest heart I can muster, thank you. Thank you for reading my words, but also thank you for believing in yourself. I hope now you believe that you don't have to have it all figured out to choose differently and that it's okay to want more. You deserve everything you desire. Now go out there and choose it. If you haven't yet, this is one final reminder to go download your FREE gift—the Choosing Fulfillment Guide.

www.theattitudeisgratitude.ca/yourguide

The guide was built to help you find the courage to choose the life you want. I hope, after reading my book, you're inspired AF to move toward that life. That inspired feeling is likely going to fade, so grab the guide and start working through some feelings!

Manufactured by Amazon.ca
Bolton, ON